W9-AFT-787

1st EDITION

Perspectives on Diseases and Disorders

HPV

Jacqueline Langwith
Book Editor

PERSPECTIVES
On Diseases & Disorders

GALE
CENGAGE Learning·

Detroit • New York • San Francisco • New Haven, Conn • Waterville, Maine • London

Elizabeth Des Chenes, *Director, Publishing Solutions*

For more information, contact:
Greenhaven Press
27500 Drake Rd.
Farmington Hills, MI 48331-3535
Or you can visit our Internet site at gale.cengage.com

For product information and technology assistance, contact us at

Gale Customer Support, 1-800-877-4253
For permission to use material from this text or product, submit all requests online at www.cengage.com/permissions

Further permissions questions can be e-mailed to permissionrequest@cengage.com

Articles in Greenhaven Press anthologies are often edited for length to meet page requirements. In addition, original titles of these works are changed to clearly present the main thesis and to explicitly indicate the author's opinion. Every effort is made to ensure that Greenhaven Press accurately reflects the original intent of the authors. Every effort has been made to trace the owners of copyrighted material.

Cover image © Paula Solloway/Alamy.

LIBRARY OF CONGRESS CATALOGING-IN-PUBLICATION DATA

HPV / Jacqueline Langwith, book editor.
    pages cm. -- (Perspectives on diseases and disorders)
  Summary: "Perspectives on Diseases and Disorders: HPV: Each volume in this timely series provides essential information on a disease or disorder (symptoms, causes, treatments, cures, etc.); presents the controversies surrounding causes, alternative treatments, and other issues"-- Provided by publisher.
  Includes bibliographical references and index.
  ISBN 978-0-7377-6355-3 (hardback)
  1. Papillomavirus diseases--Popular works. 2. Genital warts--Popular works.
I. Langwith, Jacqueline, editor of compilation.
  RC168.P15H68 2013
  616.9'11--dc23

                                                                2012040787

Printed in the United States of America
1 2 3 4 5 6 7 16 15 14 13 12

CONTENTS

FOREWORD

"Medicine, to produce health, has to examine disease."
—Plutarch

Independent research on a health issue is often the first step to complement discussions with a physician. But locating accurate, well-organized, understandable medical information can be a challenge. A simple Internet search on terms such as "cancer" or "diabetes," for example, returns an intimidating number of results. Sifting through the results can be daunting, particularly when some of the information is inconsistent or even contradictory. The Greenhaven Press series Perspectives on Diseases and Disorders offers a solution to the often overwhelming nature of researching diseases and disorders.

From the clinical to the personal, titles in the Perspectives on Diseases and Disorders series provide students and other researchers with authoritative, accessible information in unique anthologies that include basic information about the disease or disorder, controversial aspects of diagnosis and treatment, and first-person accounts of those impacted by the disease. The result is a well-rounded combination of primary and secondary sources that, together, provide the reader with a better understanding of the disease or disorder.

Each volume in Perspectives on Diseases and Disorders explores a particular disease or disorder in detail. Material for each volume is carefully selected from a wide range of sources, including encyclopedias, journals, newspapers, nonfiction books, speeches, government documents, pamphlets, organization newsletters, and position papers. Articles in the first chapter provide an authoritative, up-to-date overview that covers symptoms, causes and effects, treatments, cures, and medical advances. The second chapter presents a substantial number of opposing viewpoints on controversial treatments and other current debates relating to the volume topic. The third chapter offers a variety of personal perspectives on the disease or disorder. Patients, doctors, caregivers, and loved ones represent just some of the voices found in this narrative chapter.

Each Perspectives on Diseases and Disorders volume also includes:

- An **annotated table of contents** that provides a brief summary of each article in the volume.
- An **introduction** specific to the volume topic.
- Full-color **charts and graphs** to illustrate key points, concepts, and theories.
- Full-color **photos** that show aspects of the disease or disorder and enhance textual material.
- **"Fast Facts"** that highlight pertinent additional statistics and surprising points.
- A **glossary** providing users with definitions of important terms.
- A **chronology** of important dates relating to the disease or disorder.
- An annotated list of **organizations to contact** for students and other readers seeking additional information.
- A **bibliography** of additional books and periodicals for further research.
- A detailed **subject index** that allows readers to quickly find the information they need.

Whether a student researching a disorder, a patient recently diagnosed with a disease, or an individual who simply wants to learn more about a particular disease or disorder, a reader who turns to Perspectives on Diseases and Disorders will find a wealth of information in each volume that offers not only basic information, but also vigorous debate from multiple perspectives.

INTRODUCTION

The human papillomavirus (HPV) is not a typical television subject; however, in 2009, HPV was the subject of an episode of the crime-drama series *Law & Order*. One of the show's main characters, Detective Anita Van Buren, went to visit her doctor. The doctor informed her that she had cervical cancer that was likely caused by an HPV infection she had contracted from her former husband. Many public health advocates were happy to see HPV and its association to cervical cancer getting publicity in a prime-time television show; however, they lamented a missed opportunity to increase awareness of HPV screening: The program did not mention the topic.

HPV screening generally refers to two different kinds of tests that can signify a woman's risk for cervical cancer. One of these tests checks for the presence of human papillomavirus DNA, while the other test checks for the presence of precancerous cells in cervical tissue. Many women are familiar with the latter test—it is referred to as the Pap test or the Pap smear—and it has been around for many years. The test that checks for HPV DNA is relatively new. When people refer to HPV screening they are generally referring to the Pap test, the HPV DNA test, or both. HPV screening can be a contentious issue. Many disagreements exist over the optimal age and frequency of HPV screening for women, the availability of screening, and whether or not men should be screened for HPV.

In 2009 the American College of Obstetricians and Gynecologists (ACOG) made changes to its HPV screening guidelines. The new guidelines included the recommendation that women wait until twenty-one years of age before getting their first Pap test. Previously, the ACOG had said that teens should start getting the Pap test within three years of being sexually active. The ACOG's new recommendation, as well as similar recommendations from the American Cancer Society (ACS) and the US Preventative Services Task Force (PSTF), is based on data suggesting that while HPV infection is common among teens, the vast majority of these infections go away on their own and do not lead to cancer. In a Reuters article published shortly after the ACOG's new screening guidelines were announced, Dr. Mark Einstein, from the Albert Einstein College of Medicine, discussed why the ACOG believes it is unnecessary to screen women younger than twenty-one for HPV. Einstein said, "They have a better chance of winning the lottery than getting cancer at that age."[1] Einstein and the ACOG believe that overscreening teenage girls for HPV can cause undue stress and anxiety and lead to unnecessary treatments that can increase a teen's risk of undergoing an early labor if pregnant later in life.

Some women's health advocates have questioned the wisdom of waiting until a woman is twenty-one to begin HPV screening. In an August 2011 post on the website EmpowHER, Bonnie Diraimondo, a registered nurse, wondered whether the medical community was turning a blind eye to HPV infections. Said Diraimondo, "Has the medical community become so complacent with the high percentage of Americans becoming infected with HPV that they would introduce guidelines which delay a woman's diagnosis, thus maintaining the status quo of contagion or worse?"[2] According to Diraimondo, regardless of her age a woman has a right to know whether she is harboring a contagious and potentially cancer-causing disease, and her sexual partners have a right to know as well.

The HPV screening recommendations from ACOG, ACS, and the PSTF are also notable because for the first time, most women are advised not to get an annual Pap test. Being tested once every two years is enough for most

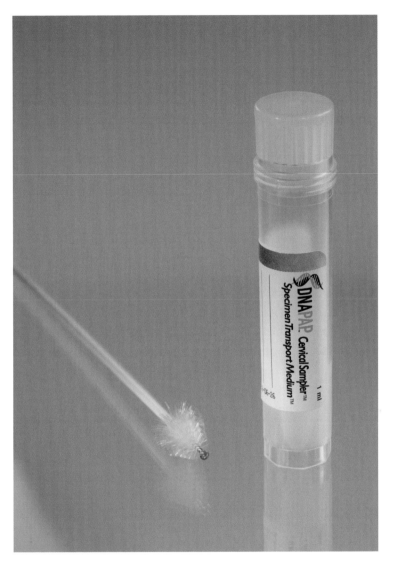

This special smear test detects HPV, which can cause cervical cancer.
(Ottfried Schreiter/ imagebroker/Alamy)

women, says the ACOG, while the ACS and PSTF recommend the Pap test once every three years. Women over thirty years of age can extend these intervals even further if they get an HPV DNA test along with the Pap test.

The organizations' rationale behind the longer intervals is the same as it is for the recommendation that women wait until age twenty-one: Most HPV infections will resolve on their own and will not develop into cancer.

According to the PSTF, "Identifying and treating lesions (infections) that will likely regress on their own does not provide a benefit large enough to outweigh the harms." The PSTF says that the harms of too much HPV screening include anxiety associated with testing positive, potential stigmatization from the diagnosis of a sexually transmitted infection, and the associated risks from additional diagnostic and treatment procedures. According to the PSTF, "Extending the interval for screening strikes the most appropriate balance between benefits and harms."[3]

Some women's health advocates contend that the issue should not be about the age screening begins or how often to screen. They think the bigger issue is the disparity in women's access to screening. Generally, research has shown that low-income and minority women tend to have less access to screening than do other women. Statistics showing that low-income and minority women are diagnosed with cervical cancer at later stages and are thus more likely to die from the disease exemplify this disparity. According to Christine Cupaiuolo, a blogger for *Our Bodies, Ourselves*, "Most women who die of cervical cancer never had regular Pap tests, had false-negative results, or did not receive proper follow-up." Cupaiuolo points to cervical cancer statistics to back up her claim. She notes that "Vietnamese immigrants are five times more likely to be diagnosed with cervical cancer than white women. African-American and Native-American women are twice as likely to die of the disease as are white women . . . and Hispanic women are 1.5 times more likely to die from cervical cancer as compared to non-Hispanic white women."[4]

While disagreements about HPV screening for women abound, men are largely left out of the discussion. There are screening tests for anal cancer called anal Pap smears, but the ACS says it does not recommend the anal Pap test because "the test has not been studied enough to know how often it should be done, or if it actually reduces the risk of anal cancer."[5] Many experts do recommend the test, however, for HIV-positive, homosexual men. There are some men's health advocates who think that the test would be beneficial for heterosexual men as well and would like to increase the test's availability.

HPV's association with cancer makes screening for it an important health issue for both women and men. In *Perspectives on Diseases and Disorders: HPV*, the contributors discuss facts related to HPV, such as HPV's transmission rates and its link to many kinds of cancer. Controversial issues surrounding HPV—including who should get the HPV vaccine and how teens should be educated about the virus—and personal stories about people whose lives have been impacted by HPV are also provided.

Notes

1. Quoted in Frederik Joelving, "No Pap Smears for Women Under 21: Guidelines," Reuters, July 21, 2010. www.reuters.com/article/2010/07/21/us-pap-smears -idUSTRE66K6AG20100721.
2. Bonnie Diraimondo, "Does Delaying Cervical and HPV Screening Have Negative Effects on Younger Women?—An Editorial," EmpowHER, August 8, 2011. www.empowher.com/cervical-cancer/content/does -delaying-cervical-and-hpv-screening-have-negative -effects-younger-women?page=0,0.
3. US Preventive Services Task Force, "Screening for Cervical Cancer," recommendation statement, March 2012. www.uspreventiveservicestaskforce.org/uspstf11 /cervcancer/cervcancerrs.htm#clinical.
4. Christine Cupaiuolo, "We Need to Increase Access to HPV Screening and Vaccinations for Underserved Women," *Our Bodies, Ourselves* (blog), January 13, 2012. www.ourbodiesourblog.org/blog/2012/01/end ing-cervical-cancer-requires-ending-disparities-in -access-to-pap-tests-and-hpv-vaccines.
5. American Cancer Society, "Anal Cancer," January 5, 2012. www.cancer.org/Cancer/AnalCancer/Detailed Guide/anal-cancer-detection.

CHAPTER 1

Understanding HPV

An Overview of Human Papillomavirus (HPV)

Warren Maltzman and Rebecca J. Frey

In the following selection Warren Maltzman and Rebecca J. Frey provide an overview of the human papillomavirus (HPV), which has become the most common sexually transmitted disease in the United States. According to the authors, about three-fourths of sexually active Americans will become infected with at least one strain of HPV at some point in their lives. Some HPV strains have relatively benign symptoms that do not lead to serious complications; however, people infected with certain strains of sexually transmitted HPV—called high-risk HPV—are at risk of developing genital warts, precancerous lesions, or cancer. One hundred percent of cervical cancer, 90 percent of anal cancer, and 40 percent of vaginal cancer is caused by high-risk HPV, the authors assert.

Maltzman is a consultant and molecular pathologist. Frey is a research and administrative associate at the East Rock Institute in New Haven, Connecticut.

Photo on facing page. The human papillomavirus is revealed in this transmission electron micrograph. (© James Cavallini/ScienceSource)

SOURCE: Warren Maltzman and Rebecca J. Frey, "Human Papilloma Virus," *Gale Encyclopedia of Medicine,* 4th edition, Laurie J. Fundukian, ed. Copyright © 2011 Cengage Learning. All rights reserved. Reproduced by permission.

HPV infection is a sexually transmitted disease (STD) caused by 30–40 of the 130 or so known strains of human papillomavirus, the name of a group of viruses that infect the skin and mucous membranes of humans and some animals. In humans these sexually transmitted strains can cause genital warts, precancerous changes in the tissues of the female vagina, or cervical cancer. Other strains of HPV are responsible for warts on the soles of the feet (plantar warts), common warts on the hands, and flat warts on the face or legs.

A Common Sexually Transmitted Disease

In recent years HPV infection has become the most common STD in the United States. Approximately 20 million Americans are infected with HPV as of 2009, and another 6.2 million people become newly infected each year. According to one study, 27 percent of women between the ages of 14 and 59 are infected with one or more types of HPV, and 35 percent of homosexual men. The Centers for Disease Control and Prevention (CDC) estimates that more than 80 percent of American women will contract at least one strain of genital HPV by age 50. About 75–80 percent of sexually active Americans of either sex will be infected with HPV at some point in their lifetime.

As far as is known, men and women are at equal risk of being infected with HPV, as are members of all races and ethnic groups.

In terms of specific illnesses associated with HPV, 11,000 women are diagnosed with cervical cancer each year in the United States and 3,900 women die of the disease. Another 5,800 women are diagnosed with cancers of the vagina and the external female genitals, while 3,300 men are diagnosed with cancer of the penis or the anal area. The risk of anal cancer is 17 to 31 times higher among gay and bisexual men than among heterosexual men.

The family of human papilloma viruses includes a large number of genetically related viruses. Many of these cause warts, including the warts commonly found on the skin. Another group of HPV preferentially infect the mucosal surfaces of the genitals, including the penis, vagina, vulva, and cervix. These are spread among adults by sexual contact. One group of HPV that infect the genitals causes soft warts, often designated condylomata acuminata. These genital warts are quite common and rarely if ever become cancerous. The most common of these low-risk HPV types are designated HPV 6 and 11.

The second group of viruses, termed high-risk HPV types, is associated with the development of cervical cancer. Individuals infected with these viruses are at higher risk for the development of precancerous lesions. Typically, infection with these viruses is common in adolescents and women in their twenties and usually do not result in cancerous growth. The most common high-risk HPV is type 16. The appearance of abnormal cells containing high-risk HPV types is seen most frequently in women over the age of 30 who have abnormal Pap smears.

It is possible that other viruses work together with human papilloma viruses to produce precancerous changes in tissue. Cases of tongue cancer have been reported in which HPV was found together with Epstein-Barr virus, or EBV. Smoking, the use of oral contraceptives for birth control for longer than five years, and suppression of the immune system are also thought to be factors that combine with HPV infection to lead to precancerous lesions in tissue.

Some people are at greater risk of sexually transmitted HPV than others:

- Gay and bisexual men.
- People with HIV or other diseases that weaken the immune system.
- Males or females below age 25. Younger people appear to be more biologically vulnerable to the HPV virus.

- People who have large numbers of sexual partners.
- People in relationships with partners who have sex with many other people.
- People who must take drugs that suppress the immune system.

HPV Causes Genital Warts and Cancer

The cause of sexually transmitted HPV infection is one or more strains of the human papillomavirus. The virus enters the body through small breaks in the skin surface or in the mucous membranes lining the genitals. In most cases the body fights off the virus within a few weeks. In some people, however, HPV remains dormant for a period ranging from a few weeks to three years in one of the lower layers of skin cells. The virus then begins to replicate (copy itself) when these cells mature and move upward to the surface of the skin. The virus affects the shape of the cells, leading to the formation of noticeable warts, precancerous changes in skin cells, or cervical cancer. About 1 percent of sexually active adults in the United States have genital warts at any one time; about 10 percent of women with high-risk HPV in the tissues of their cervix will develop long-lasting HPV infections that put them at risk for cervical cancer.

The percentages of cancers caused by high-risk types of HPV are as follows:

- Cervical cancer: 100 percent
- Anal cancer: 90 percent
- Cancer of the vulva: 40 percent
- Vaginal cancer: 40 percent
- Oropharyngeal cancer: 12 percent
- Oral cancer: 3 percent

Symptoms of sexually transmitted HPV infection may include:

- Genital warts. These appear as bumps or clusters of fleshy outgrowths around the anus or on the genitals. Some may grow into large cauliflower-shaped masses. Genital warts usually appear within weeks or months after sexual contact with an infected person. If left untreated, genital warts may go away, remain unchanged, or increase in size or number but will not turn into cancers. It is possible, however, for a person to be infected with a high-risk strain of HPV as well as one of the strains that cause genital warts; therefore the appearance of genital warts does not necessarily mean that the person is not at risk of cancer.

• Precancerous changes in the tissues of the female cervix. These are flat growths on the cervix that cannot be seen or felt by the infected woman.

• Cancer. High-risk strains of HPV can cause cancers of the mouth and throat as well as cancers of the anal area and the male and female genitals. These typically take years to develop after infection. In men, symptoms of anal cancer may include bleeding, pain, or a discharge from the anus, or changes in bowel habits. Early signs of cancer of the penis may include thickening of the skin, tissue growths, or sores.

It was not fully understood as of 2009 why most infections with high-risk HPV are of short duration, while a small percentage persist and eventually transform cervical cells to a state of cancerous growth.

Women Can Pass HPV to Their Babies During Childbirth

In addition to producing precancerous lesions in some patients, HPV infections in women are a health concern because they can be transmitted to the respiratory tract of a baby during childbirth. This type of HPV infection may lead to a rare disorder known as juvenile-onset recurrent respiratory papillomatosis (JO-RRP) or laryngeal papillomatosis, in which papillomas or warts form in the child's airway, producing hoarseness or partial blockage of the windpipe. Although laryngeal papillomatosis can occur in HPV-infected adults, 60–80 percent of cases occur in children, most of them younger than three years.

Laryngeal papillomatosis is usually diagnosed by laryngoscopy. Surgery, whether traditional or laser surgery, is the usual treatment for JO-RRP, but the warts often recur and require additional surgery to remove them. In extreme cases, the patient may be given a tracheotomy, a procedure in which a hole is cut through the throat into the windpipe and a tube is inserted to keep the breathing hole open. A new treatment for the disorder is photodynamic therapy or PDT. In PDT, a special light-sensitive dye is injected into the patient's blood. The dye collects in the tumors rather than in healthy tissue. When bright light of a specific wavelength is shined on the throat, it destroys the tumors containing the dye.

Cidofovir and interferon are often given as adjuvant [helping the primary treatment work better] treatments for this disease as of the early 2000s. JO-RRP is a serious illness, leading to death in a significant number of affected children. In a very few cases, respiratory papillomatosis can lead to cancer as well as breathing difficulties. . . .

Diagnosing HPV

There is no general blood, urine, or imaging test for HPV infection. The diagnosis of genital warts is obvious based on their location and appearance. The doctor may, however, use a vinegar solution to identify HPV-infected areas on the skin of the genitals. The vinegar solution will turn white if HPV is present. Since genital warts are caused by low-risk strains of HPV, the doctor does not need to identify the specific strain of the virus that is present.

Sexually active women should be screened periodically for the presence of changes in the tissues of the cervix. The most common test is the Papanikolaou test or Pap smear, invented by a Greek physician in the 1940s. To perform a Pap smear, the doctor takes a small spatula to obtain cells from the outer surface of the cervix and smears the collected cells on a slide that is then examined in a laboratory for signs of any abnormal cells. If abnormal or questionable cells are found, the doctor may order an HPV DNA test, which can identify the DNA of 13 high-risk types of HPV in cells taken from the cervix.

There were no HPV screening tests for men as of 2009; however, some doctors suggested that anal Pap smears for men who have sex with men would be useful in early detection of anal cancer.

The relationship among HPV, precancerous cellular changes, and cervical cancer have led to the suggestion that testing for the presence of HPV can be a useful addition to Pap smears. Pap smears involve microscopic analysis of cells removed from the cervix. The results of these tests are generally reported as either normal or consistent with the presence of cancer or a precancerous

The family of human papillomaviruses comprises a large number of genetically related viruses that include those that cause warts like these. (© CNRI/Photo Researchers, Inc.)

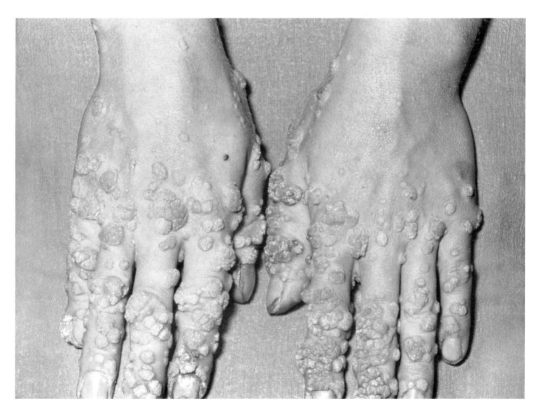

condition. Patients receiving the latter diagnosis usually are treated either by excisional or ablative therapy surgery [cutting away cancerous or precancerous tissue] or some other means in order to remove the tumor or precancerous lesion.

In some cases the cytologist or pathologist examining a Pap smear reports a "borderline" result when abnormal cells are observed, but it is not possible to distinguish whether the changes seen are due to early precancerous changes or to inflammation caused by some infectious agent or irritant. In these cases, some physicians and scientists believe that testing for the presence of HPV can help to identify those women who should be closely followed for the development of early cancerous lesions, or who should undergo colposcopy, a procedure to examine the cervix for precancerous lesions. These cancer precursors, termed cervical intraepithelial neoplasia (CIN) when identified early, before they have become invasive, can almost always be completely removed by minor surgery, essentially curing the patient before the cancer has had a chance to develop. The cervical tissue removed, which includes the precancerous tissue, is examined as part of a biopsy to confirm the diagnosis, and if requested by a doctor, can be tested for the presence of high-risk HPV types.

Treating HPV Infection

Patients with genital warts should *never* use over-the-counter preparations designed to remove common or flat warts from the hands or face. Doctors can treat genital warts with various medical or surgical techniques:

- Cryotherapy. Cryotherapy uses liquid nitrogen to freeze the warts. The dead tissue in the wart falls away from the skin beneath in about a week.
- Imiquimod. Imiquimod (Aldara) is a topical cream that gets rid of genital warts by stimulating the body's immune system to fight the virus that causes the warts.

- Podofilox. Podofilox (Condylox) is a topical medication available in liquid or gel form that destroys the wart tissue.
- Surgery. The doctor can remove the wart by drying it out with an electric needle and then scraping the tissue with a sharp instrument called a curette. Lasers can also be used to remove genital warts.

Low-grade precancerous changes in the tissue of the female cervix are not usually treated directly because most of them will eventually go away on their own without developing into cancer. The patient should, however, see the doctor for follow-up Pap smears to make sure that the tissues are returning to normal. High-risk precancerous lesions are removed, usually by surgery, cryotherapy, electrocauterization, or laser surgery.

Since the incidence of latent and recurrent infections is high, the eradication of HPV is not always 100 percent effective. It is essential to be aware that HPV is a sexually transmitted disease and women must engage in safe sex practices to decrease the risk of spreading the virus or becoming reinfected. A vaccine effective against four of the HPV types most likely to cause genital warts or cervical cancer was approved for use in 2006. . . . As of 2009, researchers were working on developing vaccines to protect against additional types of the HPV virus.

The prognosis of sexually transmitted HPV infections depends on the patient's age, number of sexual partners, gender, and the condition of his or her immune system. Women are significantly more likely than men to develop cancers following HPV infection. However, most people of either sex with normally functioning immune systems who are infected with HPV will clear the infection from their bodies within two years.

FAST FACT

The World Health Organization (WHO) estimates that every year 529,828 women are diagnosed with cervical cancer, of which 275,128 die from the disease. The WHO says that cervical cancer ranks as the third most frequent cancer in women worldwide.

The information in this graph is based on the National Health and Nutrition Examination Survey of Females Aged 14–59 years, 2003–2006. Both high-risk and low-risk HPV types were detected in some females.

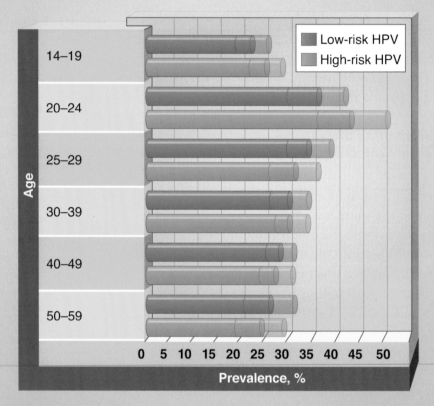

Taken from: US Centers for Disease Control and Prevention. HPV Vaccine to Prevent Cervical Cancer, June 2, 2006. www.cancer.gov/concertopics/understandingcancer/HPV-vaccine/cervix.pdf.

Prevention of HPV Infection

Preventive measures that people can take to lower their risk of HPV infection include:

- Abstaining from sex or having sex only with an uninfected partner who is faithful.
- Reducing the number of sexual partners.

- Using condoms regularly during sexual intercourse.
- For women, using a vaccine called Gardasil. Approved by the Food and Drug Administration (FDA) in 2006, Gardasil protects against the four types of HPV that cause most cervical cancers and genital warts. The vaccine is recommended for 11- and 12-year-old girls. It is also recommended for girls and women age 13 through 26 who have not yet been vaccinated or completed the vaccine series. Gardasil works best in girls who have not yet been sexually active. It is given as a series of three shots over a six-month period.

A second human papillomavirus vaccine, Cervarix, was approved in Europe, Australia, and the Philippines in 2007. It received FDA approval for use in the United States in October 2009.

In addition to giving the available preventive vaccines to women, some doctors think it might be a useful preventive measure to vaccinate men as well.

Editor's note: As of 2011, the CDC recommends the HPV vaccine for all boys and young men, both for their own protection and that of their partners.

HPV Transmission Rates Among Heterosexual Couples

Sarah C.P. Williams

In the following selection Sarah C.P. Williams discusses the importance of research on how HPV is passed from person to person. Williams talks about a 2011 study by researchers at McGill University in Montreal, Canada, that provides new insight into HPV transmission between heterosexual partners. The researchers found no difference between male-to-female and female-to-male transmission rates. They also found no link between the number of sexual partners a person has had and their chances of acquiring the virus. According to Williams, understanding how HPV spreads is important in developing policies to combat and manage the disease.

Williams is a science journalist. Her articles appear in print and online, including *Science, Nature Medicine*, and MyHealthNewsDaily .com.

SOURCE: Sarah C.P. Williams, "HPV Transmission: 20% Chance an Uninfected Partner Will Pick Up Virus," *My Health News Daily*, October 21, 2011. http://www.livescience.com. Copyright © 2011 by TechMediaNetwork, Inc. All rights reserved. Reproduced by permission.

If one person in a heterosexual couple has human papillomavirus (HPV), there's a 20 percent chance his or her partner will pick up the virus within six months, a new study concludes.

The study, the largest-yet analysis of HPV transmission rates, found no difference between male-to-female transmission rates and female-to-male transmission rates.

It also found no link between the number of partners in a person's sexual past and their chances of picking up HPV from a current partner.

"There's been very little work done on how frequently HPV transmits," said study author Ann Burchell of McGill University in Montreal. "Most of the work on HPV has revolved around how common it is within a population." Combining the data on transmission and frequency, she said, can help researchers get a fuller picture of how the virus spreads.

The new study was published Oct. 7 [2011] in the *Journal of Infectious Diseases*.

Catching a Virus

HPV infects the genitals of both males and females, and can cause genital warts as well as cervical cancer. It's the most common sexually transmitted virus in the U.S.—around 50 percent of sexually active adults will have HPV at some point in their lives. Most cases only last a year or two, but other cases can linger for longer and lead to cancer.

To study how often HPV spread from an infected person to an uninfected sex partner, Burchell recruited college-age women in relationships. She and her colleagues identified 179 couples in which one person was infected with HPV, but the other wasn't. Four months after the study began, Burchell asked the couples to return to the clinic for follow-up testing and questionnaires.

When the researchers tallied the final numbers of who had been newly infected with HPV, they found that the

HPV Is a Common Infection

Current statistics on HPV indicate that 37 out of 57 people are infected with HPV; 20 out of 31 women and 17 out of 26 men. At least 50 percent of sexually active men and women acquire a genital HPV infection at some point in their lives. By age 50, at least 80 percent of women will have been infected with genital HPV infection.

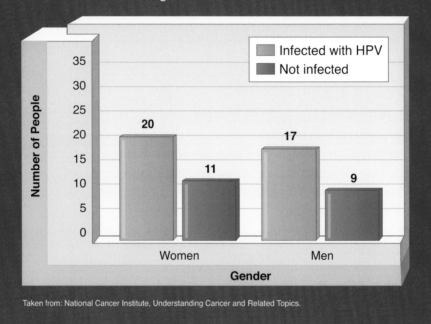

Taken from: National Cancer Institute, Understanding Cancer and Related Topics.

overall probability of transmission was 20 percent over a six-month period. The couples reported having sex four times a week, on average, and 50 percent said they never used condoms.

Other smaller studies have suggested that HPV more easily spreads from females to males than from males to females. The new study, however, saw nearly identical rates of transmission.

"Our hypothesis is that female-to-male transmission may occur more often, but results in shorter infections, and by the time we saw these couples again, some of those male infections had cleared," Burchell said.

The incremental nature of follow-up visits is a limitation of all studies that look at the natural course of a disease, said Brenda Hernandez, of the University of Hawaii Cancer Center. Hernandez has led ongoing studies looking at the transmission of HPV and how long infections last.

"Ideally, you'd want to be able to sample individuals every single day," she said.

Researchers had also previously hypothesized that those who've had many sexual partners are more likely to have gained immunity to HPV—so they were thought to be less likely to pick up a new HPV infection from a current partner. When someone is infected with a virus, the body often saves antibodies to fight off the virus in the future.

The new study, however, found no correlation between the number of sex partners and immunity.

Hernandez said HPV doesn't necessarily follow the rules when it comes to antibodies. "We've found that only a little over half of females who have an HPV infection develop antibodies," she said. This lack of antibodies could explain why few people develop natural immunity to HPV.

> **FAST FACT**
>
> Globally about 11.4 percent of women in the general population are estimated to harbor a cervical HPV infection at any given time, according to the World Health Organization.

Vaccination Against HPV

In 2006, the first vaccine against HPV was approved for use in females, and in 2009, the approval was extended to males. Understanding the transmission rates of HPV, Burchell said, can help researchers understand how the vaccine should be used to stop the spread of the virus.

The more transmissible a virus is, Burchell explained, the more people in a population that need to be vaccinated to keep the virus from spreading.

"These numbers are really important to understand for vaccine program planning," Burchell said. "The better we can understand how HPV moves around the population, the better we can control it."

Burchell said she also wants to study further the length of infections, how antibodies against HPV affect rates and whether the amount of virus in a person's body affects the likelihood of transmission. Continuing,

Around 50 percent of sexually active adults will be infected with HPV at some point in their lives. (© **Horizon International Images Limited**/Alamy)

detailed studies of larger populations are needed to fully understand how HPV spreads, said Hernandez. For example, her team has found that HPV can spread from one location on a person to another location without sexual contact.

"We still don't feel that this research is at the point where it is directly translatable to public policy on how to manage HPV," she said.

Many Treatments Exist for Genital Warts Caused by HPV

US Centers for Disease Control and Prevention

In the following selection the US Centers for Disease Control and Prevention (CDC) details the different treatment options available for genital warts. Treatments discussed by the CDC include drugs applied topically that disrupt cell division or stimulate the immune system, caustic agents, cryotherapy, and surgery. According to the CDC, these and other treatments can eliminate the presence of genital warts. The CDC is a component of the US Department of Health and Human Services. It is the nation's premier health-promotion, prevention, and preparedness agency.

T he primary reason for treating genital warts is the amelioration of symptoms (including relieving cosmetic concerns) and ultimately, removal of the warts. In most patients, treatment can induce wart-free periods. If left untreated, visible genital warts can resolve on their own, remain unchanged, or increase in size or number. Available therapies for genital warts

SOURCE: "Genital Warts," *Sexually Transmitted Diseases Treatment Guidelines 2010*, US Centers for Disease Control and Prevention, 2010.

likely reduce, but probably do not eradicate, HPV infectivity. Whether the reduction in HPV viral DNA resulting from treatment reduces future transmission remains unclear. No evidence indicates that the presence of genital warts or their treatment is associated with the development of cervical cancer.

Treatment Regimens

Treatment of genital warts should be guided by the preference of the patient, available resources, and the experience of the health-care provider. No definitive evidence suggests that any of the available treatments are superior to any other, and no single treatment is ideal for all patients or all warts. The use of locally developed and monitored treatment algorithms has been associated with improved clinical outcomes and should be encouraged. Because of uncertainty regarding the effect of treatment on future transmission of HPV and the possibility of spontaneous resolution, an acceptable alternative for some persons is to forego treatment and wait for spontaneous resolution.

Factors that influence selection of treatment include wart size, wart number, anatomic site of the wart, wart morphology, patient preference, cost of treatment, convenience, adverse effects, and provider experience. Factors that might affect response to therapy include the presence of immunosuppression and compliance with therapy, which can consist of either a single treatment or complete course of treatment. In general, warts located on moist surfaces or in intertriginous [a part of the body where two skin areas touch] areas respond best to topical treatment. The treatment modality should be changed if a patient has not improved substantially after a complete course of treatment or if side effects are severe. Most genital warts respond within 3 months of therapy. The response to treatment and any side effects should be evaluated throughout the course of therapy.

Complications occur rarely when treatment is administered properly. . . . Depressed or hypertrophic scars are uncommon but can occur, especially if the patient has had insufficient time to heal between treatments. Rarely, treatment can result in disabling chronic pain syndromes . . . or, in the case of anal warts, painful defecation or fistulas [an abnormal passageway between body parts that are not normally connected]. . . .

Treatment regimens are classified into patient-applied and provider-applied modalities. Patient-applied modalities are preferred by some patients because they can be administered in the privacy of the patient's home. To ensure that patient-applied modalities are effective, patients must comply with the treatment regimen and must be capable of identifying and reaching all genital warts. Follow-up visits are not required for persons using patient-applied therapy. However, follow-up visits after several weeks of therapy enable providers to answer any questions patients might have about the use of the medication and any side effects they have experienced; follow-up visits also facilitate the assessment of a patient's response to treatment. . . .

FAST FACT

About 25 percent of genital warts come back within three months after a treatment, according to Merck, maker of the HPV vaccine.

Podofilox is an antimitotic [prevents cell division] drug that destroys warts, is relatively inexpensive, easy to use, safe, and self-applied. Podofilox solution should be applied with a cotton swab, or podofilox gel with a finger, to visible genital warts twice a day for 3 days, followed by 4 days of no therapy. . . . Mild to moderate pain or local irritation might develop after treatment. The safety of podofilox during pregnancy has not been established.

Imiquimod is a topically active immune enhancer that stimulates production of interferon and other cytokines [proteins released by the immune system to fight infection]. Imiquimod cream should be applied once daily at bedtime, three times a week for up to 16 weeks.

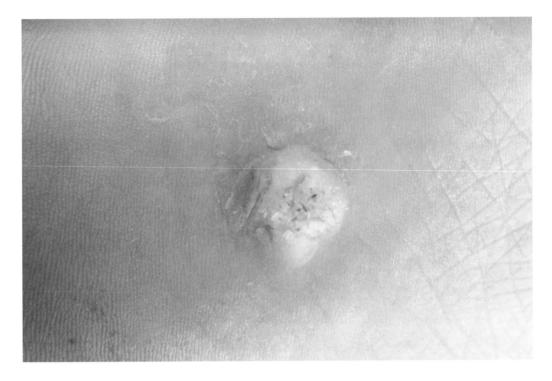

... Imiquimod might weaken condoms and vaginal diaphragms. The safety of imiquimod during pregnancy has not been established.

A genital wart (shown) is caused by HPV. (© Biophoto Associates/ Photo Researchers, Inc.)

Sinecatechin ointment, a green-tea extract with an active product (catechins [antioxidants]), should be applied three times daily ... using a finger to ensure coverage with a thin layer of ointment until complete clearance of warts. This product should not be continued for longer than 16 weeks. ... This medication may weaken condoms and diaphragms. No clinical data are available regarding the efficacy or safety of sinecatechins compared with other available anogenital wart treatment modalities. The medication is not recommended for HIV-infected persons, immunocompromised persons, or persons with clinical genital herpes because the safety and efficacy of therapy in these settings has not been established. The safety of sinecatechins during pregnancy also is unknown.

Cryotherapy [freezing] destroys warts by thermal-induced cytolysis [disintegration of cells]. Health-care providers must be trained on the proper use of this therapy because over- and undertreatment can result in complications or low efficacy. Pain after application of the liquid nitrogen [the freezing agent], followed by necrosis [tissue death] and sometimes blistering, is common. Local anesthesia (topical or injected) might facilitate therapy if warts are present in many areas or if the area of warts is large.

Podophyllin resin [caustic agent from the root of the May apple] 10%–25% should be applied to each wart

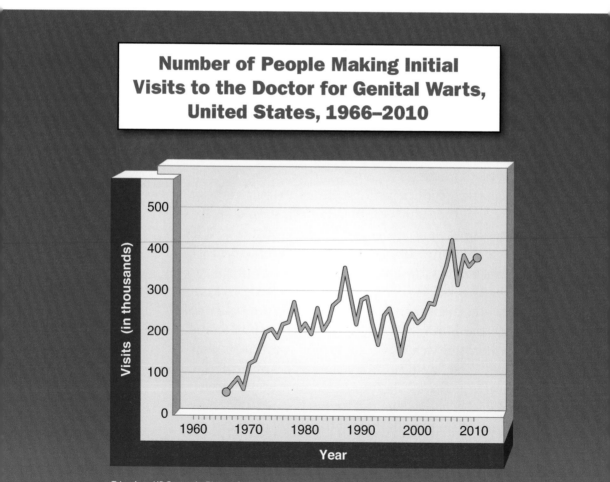

Number of People Making Initial Visits to the Doctor for Genital Warts, United States, 1966–2010

Taken from: US Centers for Disease Control and Prevention. "Sexually Transmitted Disease Surveillance," 2010. www.cdc.gov/std/stats10/slides/slides 2010.pdf.

and allowed to air-dry before the treated area comes into contact with clothing; overapplication or failure to air dry can result in local irritation caused by spread of the compound to adjacent areas. The treatment can be repeated weekly, if necessary. . . . The safety of podophyllin during pregnancy has not been established. Podophyllin resin preparations differ in the concentration of active components and contaminants. The shelf life and stability of podophyllin preparations are unknown.

Both TCA [trichloroacetic acid] and BCA [bichloroacetic acid] are caustic agents that destroy warts by chemical coagulation of proteins. Although these preparations are widely used, they have not been investigated thoroughly. TCA solutions have a low viscosity [density] comparable with that of water and can spread rapidly if applied excessively; therefore, they can damage adjacent tissues. . . .

Surgical therapy has the advantage of usually eliminating warts at a single visit. However, such therapy requires substantial clinical training, additional equipment, and a longer office visit. After local anesthesia is applied, the visible genital warts can be physically destroyed by electrocautery [a heated needle]. . . . Alternatively, the warts can be removed either by tangential excision [cutting away affected tissue] with a pair of fine scissors or a scalpel, by laser, or by curettage [scraping]. . . . Surgical therapy is most beneficial for patients who have a large number or area of genital warts. . . .

Because all available treatments have shortcomings, some clinics employ combination therapy (simultaneous use of two or more modalities on the same wart at the same time). Data are limited regarding the efficacy or risk of complications associated with use of such combinations.

HPV Is Linked to an Increase in Head and Neck Cancers

Jo Ciavaglia

In the following article Jo Ciavaglia describes a trend of increasing HPV-related throat cancers in men. Ciavaglia says that HPV is responsible for a dramatic rise in throat cancers, which historically were associated primarily with smoking or alcohol use. According to Ciavaglia, throat cancer is on track to surpass cervical cancer as the most prevalent HPV-caused cancer.

Ciavaglia is a staff writer for PhillyBurbs.com, a central website for the *Bucks County Courier Times, Burlington County Times,* and the *Intelligencer* in Doylestown in southeastern Pennsylvania.

First, Dr. Miriam Lango delivered the bad news to the wife—the biopsy confirmed cancer, one associated with the human papillomavirus [HPV], a common sexually transmitted disease.

The head and neck surgeon then explained that her husband's throat cancer wasn't evidence he was recently unfaithful.

He likely was infected decades earlier, which is typically the case with men diagnosed with throat cancer who test positive for HPV, a virus that most people associate exclusively with cervical cancer in women.

"They absolutely don't see this coming," Lango said. "It's such a new entity."

But emerging research suggests that HPV-related throat cancer is poised to become the leading form of head and neck cancer in the U.S. [An October 2011] study found that, at its current rate, throat cancer will surpass cervical cancer as the leading HPV-associated cancer in the next decade.

A malignant cancer of the throat is shown here. An increased number of head and neck cancers is attributed to HPV. (© James Cavallini/Photo Researchers, Inc.)

Doctors say the trend is worrisome because no screening test exists for HPV-related oral cancers, though the diagnosis is rising at a rate of 10 percent a year.

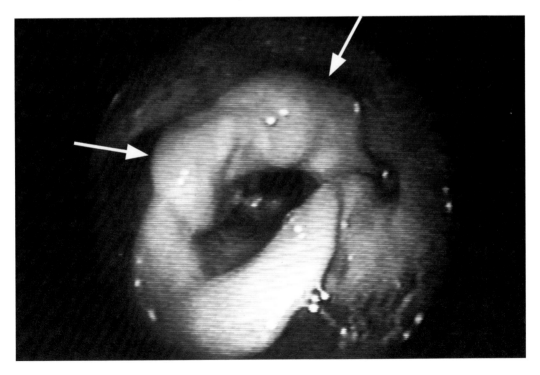

HPV is so common that at least half of sexually active people contract it at some point in their lives. About 6 million people are newly infected with the virus each year, according to the Centers for Disease Control and Prevention [CDC]. Almost all of the 12,000 cases of cervical cancer a year in the U.S. are HPV-associated.

Historically, oropharyngeal cancers have been associated with tobacco and alcohol use, but now researchers have found a link between HPV and a dramatic rise in throat cancer in patients who have neither classic risk factor.

The oropharynx is the middle part of the throat behind the mouth, and includes the base of the tongue, the side and back walls of the throat and the tonsils. Nearly 10,000 new cases of oropharyngeal cancer are diagnosed a year, according to the CDC.

Between 1984 and 1989, roughly 16 percent of cancers involving the base of the tongue and the back of the throat and tonsils were HPV-related. Today, the virus is detected in 70 percent of those cancers, which mostly are diagnosed in men, according to [an October 2011] study appearing in the *Journal of Clinical Oncology*.

"HPV infection and cancer is not just a woman's disease anymore," said Dr. Kenneth Einhorn, chief of ears-nose-throat division at Abington Memorial Hospital.

Researchers believe the rise in HPV-related throat cancer can be attributed to sexual transmission because at least 90 percent of HPV-positive throat cancers are the HPV16 strain, which is the same high-risk genotype most frequently observed in cervical cancer. But doctors have not determined if the virus also can be spread through casual saliva contact, such as kissing.

At Fox Chase Cancer Center in Philadelphia, more than a half dozen cases of HPV-related throat cancer in

FAST FACT

From 1999 through 2008 incidence rates of oropharyngeal (mouth and throat) cancers in the United States increased by 4.4 percent per year among white men, according to data compiled by the North American Association of Central Cancer Registries.

HPV-Related Throat Cancer Rates by State

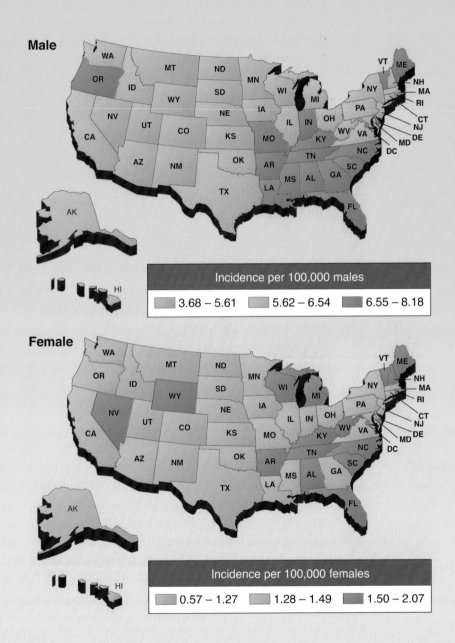

Male

Incidence per 100,000 males

3.68 – 5.61   5.62 – 6.54   6.55 – 8.18

Female

Incidence per 100,000 females

0.57 – 1.27   1.28 – 1.49   1.50 – 2.07

Taken from: US Centers for Disease Control and Prevention, Division of Cancer Prevention and Control, April 18, 2012. www.cdc.gov/cancer/hpv/statistics/state/oropharyngeal.htm.

men are diagnosed monthly, a rate that has accelerated over the last five years, said Lango, the head and neck surgeon.

But the connection is something that Lango only recently picked up on after noticing an uptick in throat cancer patients who didn't fit the typical profile. They were men in their 40s or early 50s, nonsmokers with families. It didn't make sense.

"For them, they wonder, what did I do?" she said. "We couldn't find a reason, but we were trying to look for it."

At first, Lango suspected the cancer was the result of secondhand smoke exposure, but then she noticed these younger patients responded unusually well to traditional cancer treatments, something that usually doesn't happen with throat cancer.

Then, last year Lango reviewed 180 patient records and found that the number with HPV-related oropharyngeal cancer nearly doubled between 1993 and 2004 at Fox Chase, while the number of patients with other throat cancers declined.

Today, she estimates as many as nine out of 10 throat cancer patients she treats test positive for HPV.

But unlike cervical cancer, little has been done in the way of screening or prevention for HPV-related throat cancers, doctors said.

Also unclear is whether Gardasil, the only cervical cancer vaccine with federal Food and Drug Administration approval for use in males, would protect against HPV-related throat cancer.

The vaccine targets the HPV16 strain, but the FDA has approved its use in males between 9 and 26 years old to reduce the risk of HPV-related genital warts and anal cancer. Doctors such as Lango believe the FDA should insist on further testing sooner, rather than later.

"The fact that we are predicting that throat cancer will become more common than cervical cancer—that should really make us concerned," she said.

CHAPTER 2

Controversies Concerning HPV

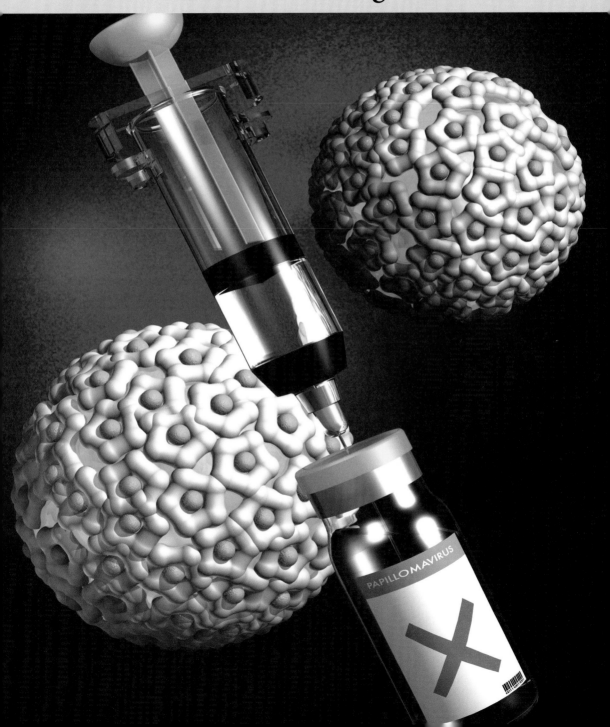

The HPV Vaccine Is Safe and Effective

US Centers for Disease Control and Prevention

In the following viewpoint the US Centers for Disease Control and Prevention (CDC) asserts that the HPV vaccine is safe and effective in preventing four types of HPV infection. The CDC and the Food and Drug Administration (FDA) are responsible for monitoring the safety of vaccines in the United States. Based on this monitoring, the CDC has found that the HPV vaccine may cause mild to moderate side effects. The reported data do not suggest that the vaccine is responsible for causing any serious adverse effects.

The US Centers for Disease Control and Prevention (CDC) is a component of the US Department of Health and Human Services and is the nation's premier health-promotion, prevention, and preparedness agency.

W*hat human papillomavirus (HPV) vaccines are available in the United States?*

Two HPV vaccines are licensed by the FDA [Food and Drug Administration] and recommended by CDC [Centers for Disease Control and Prevention].

Photo on previous page. Whether HPV vaccines are safe is the subject of much debate. (© BSIP/ Photo Researchers, Inc.)

SOURCE: "Frequently Asked Questions about HPV Vaccine Safety," US Centers for Disease Control and Prevention, August 8, 2011.

These vaccines are Cervarix (made by GlaxoSmithKline) and Gardasil (made by Merck).

What are the known side effects of the HPV vaccines?

The most common side effects are pain and redness where the shot is given (in the arm). About 1 person in 10 will get a mild fever (less than 100.4°F). About 1 person in 30 will get itching where they got the shot. About 1 person in 60 will experience a moderate fever (less than or equal to 100.4°F to less than 102.2°F). These symptoms do not last long and go away on their own.

What is an adverse event?

An adverse event is a health problem that occurs after someone receives a vaccine or medicine. It may or may not have been caused by the vaccine or medicine. For example, the person might get a headache after getting a vaccine. This might be caused by the vaccine or it might be caused by something else.

How was the safety of the HPV vaccines studied before they were licensed?

HPV vaccines were studied in clinical trials and found to be safe before they were licensed. For Gardasil, over 29,000 males and females participated in these trials. Cervarix was studied in over 30,000 females participating in several clinical trials performed all over the world.

Who is in charge of monitoring the safety of vaccines in the U.S.?

Working with healthcare providers throughout the United States, two government agencies, the Food and Drug Administration (FDA) and the Centers for Disease Control and Prevention (CDC), monitor the safety of vaccines. Vaccine manufacturers also often monitor vaccine safety after a product is already approved and on the market.

How do the FDA and the CDC monitor the safety of vaccines after they are licensed?

There are 3 systems used to monitor the safety of vaccines after they are licensed and being used in the U.S.

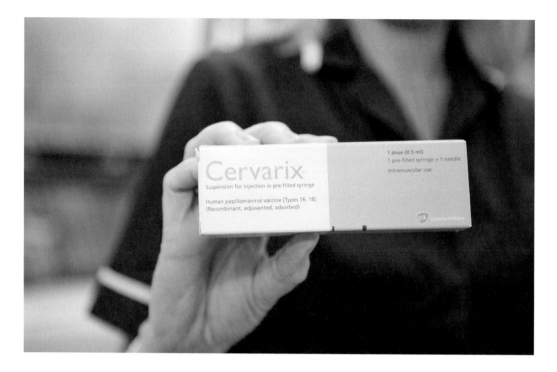

Cervarix HPV vaccine is one of two vaccines licensed by the FDA for prevention of cervical cancer.
(© Dr. P. Marazzi/Photo Researchers, Inc.)

These systems can monitor side effects already known to be caused by vaccines as well as detect rare adverse events that were not identified during a vaccine's clinical trials.

• The Vaccine Adverse Event Reporting System (VAERS) receives reports of health problems following vaccination, called "adverse events". VAERS reports can be entered online, or sent by regular mail or fax. Reports can be made by doctors, parents, or family members, someone who got a vaccine, or by a manufacturer. Reports can be submitted at any time after someone gets a vaccine. This means a person can report a health problem that develops months or even years after they get a vaccine. All reports are reviewed by trained staff at both FDA and CDC. VAERS can detect patterns in reports to show that a vaccine *might* be the cause of the adverse event (a possible side effect). It cannot be used to determine definitively if the vaccine caused the adverse event.

- The Vaccine Safety Datalink (VSD) is a collaboration between CDC and several managed care organizations [health care systems based on cost-cutting efforts] with advanced electronic health records. The VSD works to address gaps in knowledge about rare and serious adverse events that may happen after someone gets a vaccine. The VSD can be used to further study health events detected by VAERS to help determine if a vaccine is causing the adverse event.
- The Clinical Immunization Safety Assessment (CISA) Network is a project between CDC and several academic medical centers in the U.S. which conduct research on adverse events that might be caused by vaccines.

What sorts of mild to moderate adverse events have been reported?

The majority of reported adverse events following HPV vaccination have been considered minor. Reports have included pain and swelling at the injection site, fever, dizziness, and nausea. Reports of people fainting have also been received.

Fainting is common after injections, especially in pre-teens and teens. Falls that occur after someone faints can cause serious injuries, such as head injuries. To help prevent injuries, CDC and FDA recommend sitting or lying down for 15 minutes after vaccination.

FAST FACT

According to the US Centers for Disease Control and Prevention, 35 million doses of the HPV vaccine were administered in the United States from 2006 through June 2011.

What sorts of serious adverse events [1] have been reported?

Guillain-Barré Syndrome (GBS), which is a rare disorder that causes muscle weakness, has been reported. To date, there is no evidence that Gardasil causes GBS.

People have reported blood clots after getting Gardasil. These clots have occurred in the heart, lungs, and

---

1. An adverse event, as defined by the Code of Federal Regulations, is considered serious if it is life threatening, or results in death, a persistent or significant disability or incapacity, congenital anomaly or birth defect, hospitalization, or prolongation of existing hospitalization.

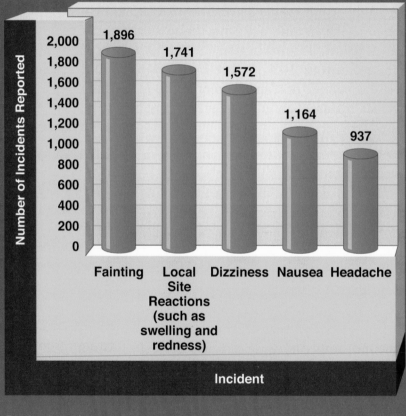

Most Common Reported Side Effects of the Gardasil Vaccine

These figures reflect incidents reported to the Vaccine Adverse Event Reporting System (VAERS) from June 1, 2006, through December 31, 2008; during this time period, 23 million doses were administered.

Number of Incidents Reported

Fainting	Local Site Reactions (such as swelling and redness)	Dizziness	Nausea	Headache
1,896	1,741	1,572	1,164	937

Incident

Taken from: Barbara Slade et al. "Postlicensure Safety Surveillance for Quadrivalent Human Papillomavirus Recombinant Vaccine." *Journal of American Medical Association*, 2009.

legs. Most (over 90%) of these people had a risk of getting blood clots, such as [from] smoking, obesity or taking oral contraceptives (the birth control pill).

Some deaths have been reported to VAERS. All reports of death are reviewed by medical doctors at the

CDC or FDA. There have been no patterns of death reports that would suggest they were caused by the vaccine.

How do you know if a serious adverse event was caused by the vaccine?

VAERS staff people receive reports of many types of events that occur after immunization. Some of these events may occur in the time period following vaccination by chance, and some may actually be caused by vaccination. VAERS staff members are trained to examine the details of each case and to look for patterns [among] cases. Such patterns might require further study by the Vaccine Safety Datalink.

Have FDA and CDC changed any recommendations for the use of HPV vaccines based on their vaccine safety monitoring?

No vaccine or medicine is completely without risk. CDC and FDA have reviewed all of the safety information available to them on Cervarix and Gardasil. CDC and FDA have determined that Gardasil is safe to use for preventing HPV types 6, 11, 16, and 18 and Cervarix is safe to use for preventing HPV types 16 and 18.

CDC continues to recommend the vaccination of 11 and 12 year old girls with 3 doses of vaccine to prevent the types of HPV that most commonly cause cervical cancer and genital warts. The vaccine is also recommended for girls and women ages 13 through 26 who did not get any or all of the doses when they were younger.

Additionally, Gardasil protects males against most genital warts. This vaccine is also recommended and available for boys and men, 9 through 26 years of age.

FDA has changed Gardasil's prescribing information to include information about preventing falls from fainting after vaccination. CDC has taken steps to remind doctors and nurses about this same information.

The HPV Vaccine Is Not Safe or Effective

Josh Axe

In the following viewpoint Josh Axe contends that the HPV vaccine is unnecessary and harmful and may even increase cervical cancer rates. According to Axe, the vaccine is unnecessary because most of the time an HPV infection will clear up on its own. He says the vaccine is harmful because it has serious side effects, including Guillain Barré syndrome, blood clots, and paralysis. He also contends that there is reason to believe that Gardasil can increase a woman's risk of developing precancerous lesions.

Axe is a health and wellness adviser, a chiropractor, and a founder of the Exodus Health Center in Nashville, Tennessee. He provides health and wellness information on a nationally syndicated radio show and on his website.

If you're the parent of a teenage or preteen girl you've undoubtedly heard about the HPV vaccine. Whether at the doctor's office or amongst other parents this is one of the latest vaccines being 'pushed' (and in some unfortunate states made mandatory) on young girls and their unknowing parents.

According to the Centers for Disease Control and Prevention (CDC) some 20 million Americans are infected right now with HPV. This high number is what many of the drug companies and doctors are using to scare parents and their daughters into getting the HPV vaccine. Don't be scared—at least not yet.

Before you opt for this vaccine it's vital to get the real facts about it. The HPV vaccine may not protect you from cancer at all and can lead to many debilitating side effects.

Doctors, drug companies, and even some in the government (Texas' own Governor Rick Perry) are advocating that this controversial vaccine is placed onto the 'mandatory' list for all young girls. These proponents of the vaccine state that it will prevent these young women from getting cervical cancer but is that the real reason? In a minute I'll tell you what the Food and Drug Administration (FDA) doesn't want you to know about the HPV vaccine and its link to cervical cancer that it supposedly protects against.

All of us know girls in their teens or twenties. Whether it's a daughter, sister, niece, or cousin these girls are going to find this vaccine pushed on them if they haven't already. It's vital to get them and their parents informed about the facts on the HPV vaccine.

First let's talk about what exactly HPV is and if you should be worried about it.

HPV: Just the Facts

Human papillomavirus or HPV is the most common sexually transmitted infection according to the Centers for Disease Control and Prevention (CDC.) There are forty types of HPV infecting both women and men. The most common spot for infection is on the genitals of either sex but it can also infect the mouth and throat. It is possible to get more than one type of HPV at a time.

HPV is passed to another through sexual contact—genital contact or oral sex—which then determines where the infection occurs. HPV can also, but rarely, be passed on to a pregnant woman's baby, resulting in Juvenile-Onset Recurrent Respiratory Papillomatosis or JORRP.

This is where it gets dangerous to protect against HPV as it usually shows no signs or symptoms in most infected people. In fact, most people infected with HPV don't even know they have it. And according to the CDC there are 6 million new cases every year. The CDC goes on to state that fifty percent of sexually active people will become infected with HPV over their lifetimes.

Those infected with HPV who do show symptoms generally show one of the two following symptoms: genital warts [and/or] Cervical cancer. If the infection is in the mouth or throat there are sometimes warts found in either or both of these places. HPV impacts normal healthy cells and makes them become abnormal. This abnormality has been thought to lead to cancers, in this case specifically cervical cancer. Previously HPV has been reported to be the leading cause of cervical cancer. This may not be true. But we'll discuss that later.

Parents and teen girls are being told that the HPV vaccine will prevent them from contracting HPV but this isn't necessarily true. One of the main HPV vaccines used, Gardasil, protects against only four of the forty known types of HPV (6, 11, 16, 18.)

And what most of us aren't told is that the body already has a perfect treatment in place for HPV. And the CDC even says that ninety percent of HPV infections simply clear on their own, without drugs or treatment of any kind.

If a person tests positive for HPV, the course of action is to determine which type they have and then use the Pap test to look for abnormality in the cells. If abnormalities are found there are various treatment options.

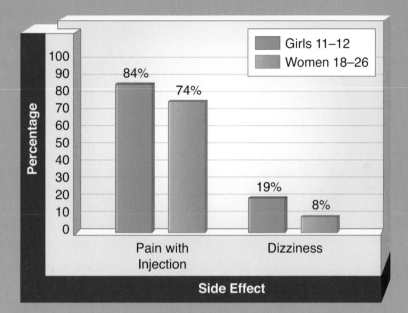

Young Girls Are More Likely than Adult Women to Report Side Effects After HPV Vaccine

These statistics are based on a survey of 3,490 Oregon and Washington girls and women who had the vaccine between February and September 2008.

Taken from: Kaiser Permanente Center for Health Research. "Young Girls More Likely to Report Side Effects After HPV Vaccine," April 3, 2012.

So on the surface it may sound like the HPV vaccine is simply an unnecessary, harmless vaccine being pushed on the public. Unnecessary? Yes. Harmless? Think again.

Dangerous Side Effects from HPV Vaccine

Those who have opted to get the HPV vaccine may now wish they didn't. This vaccine has some serious side effects that have been reported to the VAERS (Vaccine Adverse Event Reporting System.)

According to the Judicial Watch, a Washington D.C. based watchdog group, VAERS has received eighteen reported deaths from the HPV vaccine, Gardasil. As of May 11, 2007, there were 1,637 reports to VAERS of adverse reactions, 371 were serious. These serious side effects that have been reported to VAERS include:

- Guillain Barré Syndrome
- Blood clots
- Fainting
- Seizures
- Spontaneous abortion
- Neurology problems
- Bells palsy
- Paralysis

The fainting is such a common side effect that doctors are now being told to have their patients lie down for at least fifteen minutes after the vaccine is administered.

But that's not the only danger when it comes to HPV vaccines.

It's recently come into light that the FDA may now know that there is not a connection between HPV and cervical cancer. If this is in fact the case these vaccines touted as preventing cervical cancer are useless. But what's of even greater concern is that there are documents previously posted by the FDA that reveal Gardasil can actually increase certain women and young girls' risk of developing precancerous lesions by a whopping 44.6 percent.

Now stay with me a minute while I try to explain this to you. A company called HiFi DNA has been pushing the FDA to classify its [HiFi DNA's] testing device for HPV to a Class II rather than a Class III device.

FAST FACT

According to data from the US National Immunization Survey, the percentage of girls aged thirteen through seventeen who received all three doses of the HPV vaccine increased from 26.7 percent in 2009 to 32.0 percent in 2010.

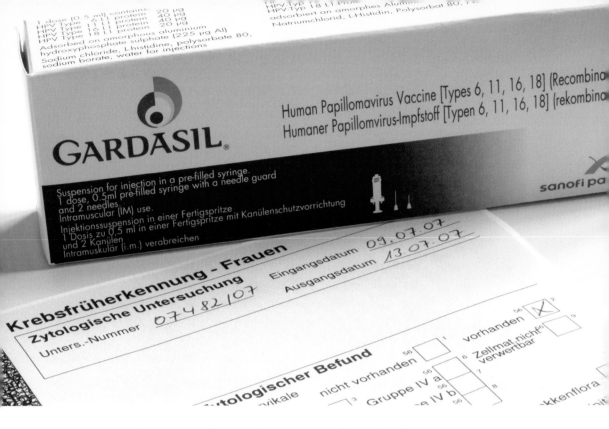

The Centers for Disease Control and Prevention and the Food and Drug Administration have determined that the vaccine Gardasil (shown) is safe for certain types of HPV and can protect against most genital warts. (© imagebroker/Alamy)

Class III devices are devices that are not allowed to be sold to the public. Class II devices are ones that the FDA more or less says may or may not be completely safe but will allow its sale to the public.

So what does this have to do with HPV and cervical cancer?

Based on HiFi DNA's submitted docket petitioning the FDA to change its portable HPV testing device from a Class III device to a Class II device the company cites the FDA's own research stating that HPV is not a cause of cervical cancer.

And HiFi DNA asserts that the FDA's own research has shown that Gardasil will increase some females' risk of developing dangerous precancerous lesions by 44.6 percent.

HiFi DNA cites the FDA news release of March 31, 2003 where the FDA in part states the following: "Most infections (by HPV) are short-lived and not associated with cervical cancer." . . .

Real Treatment and Prevention of HPV

So if the vaccine for HPV prevention is a scam, which the mounting evidence clearly points to, as well as being dangerous for certain young girls and women, then what's the solution?

The only way that HPV is spread is through sexual contact. One of the best ways to avoid contracting HPV is to use condoms. Another is to limit your sexual partners or abstain from sex until you're married or in a long term serious relationship. While these standards have seemed to all but vanish, society could use a return to them.

The increase in sexually transmitted diseases is a clue that maybe society as a whole should re-think the way we approach sex and intimacy.

But if you do come down with HPV what can you do? As I mentioned earlier, ninety percent of HPV infections resolve themselves within two years. If you boost your body's own healing mechanisms by eating healthy, getting plenty of sleep, exercising, keeping stress low, and living an overall healthy lifestyle, HPV will most likely go away on it's own.

Don't get drawn into the HPV scare. Do your own research, get the facts, and do what's the best to protect your loved ones or yourself from HPV. In my opinion, a vaccine is definitely not the best answer.

The Government Should Mandate the HPV Vaccine

Amanda Marcotte

In the following viewpoint Amanda Marcotte takes issue with what she calls the "right-wing rumor mill" regarding the HPV vaccine, and explains why she thinks the government should mandate this vaccination. According to Marcotte, the vaccine should be mandated because of the widespread nature of HPV infection and its potential to cause serious medical problems and death. She says that sometimes the government must act to protect public health, such as by prohibiting drunk driving and speeding. Mandating the HPV vaccination is the only way to protect the public from the harms of HPV. In addition, once the vaccine is administered to all and shown to be safe and effective, right-wing fear mongering will be ineffective, says Marcotte.

Marcotte is a journalist, opinion writer, and author of two books: *It's a Jungle Out There: The Feminist Survival Guide to Politically Inhospitable Environments* and *Get Opinionated*.

Laura Bassett at the *Huffington Post* has an excellent, must-read rundown of the whole controversy over the HPV vaccine that's been stirred up with [conservative Republican congresswoman] Michele Bachmann's ignorant statements [of September, 2011] about it. I wish everyone would read this; it addresses much of the confusion that has leaked into the public because the abstinence-only fanatics have been studiously spreading

Conservative congresswoman Michele Bachmann (shown) was criticized for stating that HPV vaccines were unsafe and caused mental retardation. (© Scott Olson/Getty images)

misinformation. I've been alarmed at how many liberals I've spoken to, online and off, who heard from somewhere that the vaccine is "untested" and that it's somehow less safe than every other vaccine on the market. In reality, it's been shown to be, both in medical tests and in the information gathered from widespread vaccination, as safe as other vaccines. That's the power that the rumor mill can have when it comes to things like this; it can create unease in people who may balk at a more blatant argument that you deserve to get HPV if you aren't a virgin who marries a virgin (and that apparently means a "kissing" virgin as well).

FAST FACT

In 2007 Texas became the first state to mandate the HPV vaccine by Governor Rick Perry's executive order. The Texas Legislature, however, later overturned the order.

HPV Vaccine Does Not Promote Teen Sexual Activity

The most damage that the right wing rumor mill has done to the HPV vaccine is they've managed to convince people, even liberals, that the vaccine is somehow a ceremonial introduction to adult sexuality. But from what I understand, the rationale for giving it to 6th graders was that it's a young enough age that it doesn't have to be that. (There's also some medical reasons that involve maximizing the effectiveness of it.) We're still in the habit in this country of thinking that sexual health care and self-awareness should start after sexual initiation, especially for women. It's getting better than it used to be in many ways; for instance, the notion that virgins can't use tampons, which was widespread when I was young, seems to have declined significantly. It also used to be typical for teenagers to lose their virginity and then start considering their contraceptive strategy, but now the majority of teenagers use some kind of contraception the first time they have sex. Conservative fears that virgins familiarizing themselves with contraception and having condoms on themselves in case they want to have

Pediatricians Generally Support the HPV Vaccine

The percentage of pediatricians who agree with the following statements:

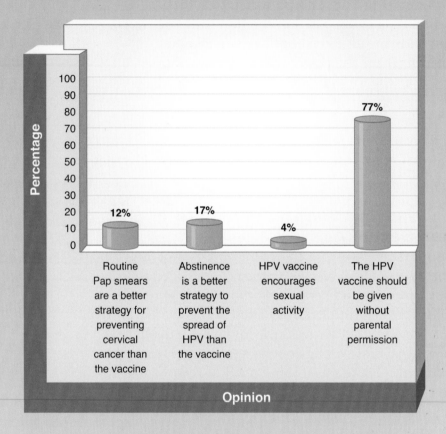

Taken from: K. Ishibashi, et al. "Pediatricians Are More Supportive of the Human Papillomavirus Vaccine than the General Public." *Southern Medical Journal*, December 2008.

sex would increase the rate of teenage sexual activity have been proven completely wrong. The Guttmacher Institute has demonstrated that kids are actually waiting longer for sex than they did in the past. I suspect that sending the message that sex is something you plan for, instead of something that you do spontaneously and then deal with, probably influences the decision to wait longer.

Why the Vaccine Should Be Required

Because HPV is widespread, nearly inevitable if you're not vaccinated, and has the potential to create medical problems or even kill you, it really should be mandated. I prefer as a rule to err on the side of freedom, but when it comes to public health issues, the government often has to get involved. Human beings struggle to weigh the risks and benefits of certain choices already—which is why we have lung cancer, unintended pregnancy, and nutrition-related diseases—and it only gets worse when you introduce the argument that you should participate in a behavior for the common good as well as your own. That's why we have laws against drunk driving and speeding, because people foolishly tend to think of their driving choices as an individual issue, instead of a common good one. Same with vaccinations. History has shown that people overrate the dangers of getting them, underrate the dangers of not getting them, and blow off their responsibilities not to spread disease (or at least have blanched at the idea that they should suffer a minor pinprick in order to help establish herd immunity). Unfortunately, the only real way to protect the populace against disease is mandating vaccinations, because human nature is flawed in such a way that voluntary vaccinations just don't cut it. History also shows that, by and large, the populace stops resisting mandates soon after they're put into place, probably because their worst fears don't come to pass and they simply forget they were worried in the first place. So it should be with HPV. Mandating it will result in a negative result of nothing, taking the steam out of right wing fear-mongering.

The Government Should Not Mandate the HPV Vaccine

Denise Hunnell

In the following viewpoint Denise Hunnell argues that the HPV vaccine should not be government mandated. According to Hunnel, mandatory HPV vaccination will erode parental rights and the integrity of the family. Some parents are opposed to having their children receive a vaccine for a sexually transmitted disease, she says. The decision about whether a child should be vaccinated for HPV should rest with parents and not the government, says Hunnel.

Hunnell is a medical doctor and a fellow at Human Life International America, a Catholic educational organization.

The *Washington Post* editorial [of September 13, 2011,] criticizing Michele Bachmann for her objections to requiring Human Papilloma Virus (HPV) vaccination for school attendance suggests that objection to this requirement would lead to a public health apocalypse following widespread rejection of other vaccines—those against polio, chicken pox, measles and other diseases. This claim is highly debatable, but even so, the editors' criticism misses the point. The resistance to mandatory vaccination is not due primarily to fear of the vaccine itself, but is rather based on an objection to the erosion of parental rights by the state. The integrity of the family must be respected.

To Want to Prevent Disease Is Reasonable

Mandatory vaccinations as a prerequisite for school attendance have traditionally been based on the reasonable desire to prevent diseases likely to be spread in the school setting. Measles, mumps, chicken pox, diphtheria, pertussis and polio are all risks among an un-vaccinated school age population.

There is, on the other hand, a precedent for vaccinating against a disease associated with risky adult behavior: the hepatitis B vaccine prevents a virus that is transmitted sexually or via contact with blood and body fluids. It is a significant risk for IV drug abusers, but it is also a risk for health care workers and emergency first-responders. This vaccine series is now initiated in newborns and is required in many school districts.

This is a reasonable precaution, mandated because teachers, emergency personnel, and students are at risk of contact with blood and other bodily fluids if an infected student becomes ill or injured. HPV, on the other hand, is *only transmitted via sexual contact*. There is, one assumes, no reason to expect exposure to HPV in a school setting.

Risks Do Not Justify Mandatory Vaccination

In a separate *Washington Post* editorial [on September 15, 2011], Michael Gerson argues that the public health

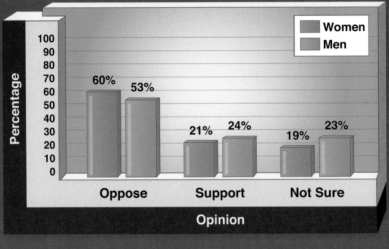

Most Americans Oppose Requiring That Sixth Grade Girls Be Vaccinated Against HPV

Taken from: Daily Kos/SEIU Weekly State of the Nation Poll, September 15–September 18, 2011. www.dailykos.com/weeklypolling/2011/9/15.

consequences of failing to vaccinate for HPV warrant state intrusion into family health care decisions. This position is not backed up by the facts. Contrary to the hype, this vaccine does not prevent "cancer;" it prevents a sexually transmitted disease: human papillomavirus (HPV). It is true that most cases of cervical cancer are linked to an infection with HPV, but prevention of cervical cancer is a secondary, not primary, effect of the vaccine. Women who are vaccinated against HPV are still advised to get regular pap smears to screen for cervical cancer.

Although HPV is the most prevalent sexually transmitted disease, the vaccine only protects against a small fraction of the subtypes of HPV. Also, most cases of HPV infection, including those caused by the cancer-causing

PERSPECTIVES ON DISEASES AND DISORDERS

subtypes, are cleared by the body naturally without medical intervention. Regular screening for cervical cancer by pap smear catches most cancers when they are easily treated. Currently, most deaths from cervical cancer occur in women who have not had regular screening or in women with underlying immunodeficiency diseases like HIV/AIDS.

It is true as well that some parents may object to the vaccination because they fear it undermines their moral instructions. Why should they, so the argument goes, have to pay for an expensive vaccination (estimated cost is $360 for the required 3-shot series) when they are teaching their children to avoid the only kind of behavior that might make them susceptible to HPV infection? Furthermore, why should their 11-year-old be *forced to undergo* vaccination for a disease that is uniquely sexually-transmitted? It is not unreasonable to conclude that the benefit to an 11-year-old is not worth the risk of the vaccine.

Nonetheless, taking precautions against untoward circumstances does not necessarily compromise the parent's efforts to encourage their children to be chaste. Just as I hope my children are never exposed to hepatitis B, I hope they are never exposed to HPV, and I will discourage the risky behaviors that might lead to either. Despite our best efforts, however, our children will not always adhere to our guidance and may choose to engage in sexual activity before marriage (not to mention the unthinkable tragedy of rape). It is also possible that they marry someone who carries the virus from a previous exposure.

FAST FACT

As of May 2012, Virginia was the only state to mandate the HPV vaccine, according to the National Conference for State Legislatures.

And so the decision to vaccinate for HPV might be a reasonable one—as might the decision to avoid vaccination. The point that the editorial board of *The Washington Post* and Michael Gerson have both missed, is that the public health risks of HPV infection do not rise to the

Michael Gerson (pictured) claimed that there would be public health consequences for failing to mandate HPV vaccination.
(© Chris Usher/CBS/Landov)

level necessary to justify mandatory vaccination. Not everything that is good for us must be a government mandate. Flu shots, exercise, and eating our green beans are all good ideas but not legal requirements. The choice of whether to vaccinate against HPV or not should remain with parents, not the state.

Boys Should Be Vaccinated for HPV

Amy Davidson

In the following viewpoint Amy Davidson asserts that it is a no-brainer that boys should receive the HPV vaccination. Davidson discounts vaccination opponents, whether they are opposed to vaccines generally, or the HPV vaccine specifically. In Davidson's view, the HPV vaccine protects men and women from cancer, and that is reason enough for boys to receive it.

Davidson is a senior editor at the *New Yorker* and writes the *Close Read* blog for the magazine's website.

The headline in the [*New York*] *Times* said, "Panel Endorses HPV Vaccine for Boys of 11." I have one of those at home—a boy that age, not a panel or a vaccine—and so my first reaction was: Sign us up! My second was annoyance that anyone would regard that as a controversial decision. The panel is the C.D.C.'s [Centers for Disease Control and Prevention] Advisory Committee

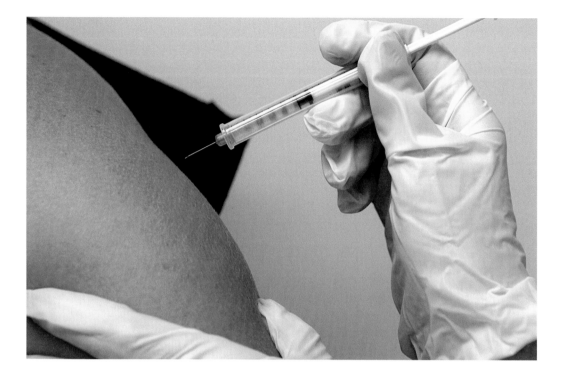

A Centers for Disease Control and Prevention panel found that HPV vaccination of boys may also provide indirect protection for girls. (© Sharon Gekoski-Kimmel/MCT/Landov)

on Immunization Practices. HPV is a virus that causes several kinds of cancer; the vaccine will save lives, maybe that of my son or someone he cares about. It will not, as [congresswoman] Michele Bachmann claimed at a Republican debate, with a lack of responsibility that was stunning even for her, cause mental disabilities. What's not to like?

Vaccine Denialism

The HPV vaccine's troubles are the result of a bad mixture of vaccine denialism—particularly, the unfounded view that immunization is linked to autism . . . —and of sexual denialism. HPV is most frequently spread by sex; the cancers are in parts of the body like the cervix, vulva, anus, mouth, and throat; the vaccine is most effective before sexual activity begins, which means giving it to children who may still be mortified by the idea of even "liking" someone. Put these together and you have Bachmann and others talking about shocking things being done in the doctor's office to "innocent little girls," as if the inoculation would turn them into Fembots. (As Ryan Lizza wrote [in the September 13, 2011, *New Yorker*], Bachmann's rhetoric "may have left uninformed listeners wondering if the vaccination involved some kind of sexual procedure.")

But what about boys? The most common cancer associated with HPV is cervical, which is why, until now, the C.D.C. only had a "recommendation"—the word has insurance implications—for girls (while saying that it was fine for boys, too). The *Times* article, by Gardiner Harris, says that "controversy is likely to intensify with the committee's latest recommendation since many of the cancers in men result from homosexual sex." It is probably sadly true that we are in for some awful rhetoric—including from people who talk about "curing" homosexuality—but it's still dismaying. Have we learned nothing from the AIDS epidemic? Or, for that matter, from a century of public-health victories tied to vaccines?

Protecting Men *and* Women

Vaccinating boys keeps them from getting sick, and that may be the main way this is sold. But, as the C.D.C. panel noted, it "may also provide indirect protection of women." One would think that raising boys to be men who protect women (and other men), directly or indirectly, would be a conservative priority as well. The maddening thing about vaccine opponents is the way they rely on the immunity of most of us, while facilitating new outbreaks of obsolete diseases. (I've written before about how scared I was when I was pregnant, and my doctor found that my rubella immunity had faded, that I would run into children whose parents had let them run around without the M.M.R. [measles, mumps, and rubella] vaccine. Unlike

> **FAST FACT**
>
> The incidence rate of HPV-associated oropharyngeal (the part of the throat at the back of the mouth) cancer in males is more than four times greater than that in females (6.2 per 100,000 males versus 1.4 per 100,000 females), according to US Centers for Disease Control and Prevention data from 2004–2008.

Incidence Rates for HPV–Associated Cancers in American Men

Cancer Site	Average Number of Cases Per Year
Penis	987
Anus	1,561
Oropharynx (the part of the throat at the back of the mouth)	8,530

These figures are based on data from 2003 to 2007.

Taken from: US Centers for Disease Control and Prevention. "Human Papillomavirus (HPV)–Associated Cancers."

the vaccine that prevents it, prenatal exposure to rubella, also known as German measles, really can cause mental disabilities.)

"This is cancer, for Pete's sake," William Schaffner, a Vanderbilt professor who worked with the panel, told Harris. "A vaccine against cancer was the dream of our youth." A dream of our youth, frustrated, perhaps, by distorted fantasies about the country's youth, and what this means for them. Isn't our dream of and for our youth that they grow up to be adults—healthy, safe, and responsible?

Boys Should Not Receive the HPV Vaccine

Jeanne Lenzer

In the following viewpoint Jeanne Lenzer argues against vaccinating boys for HPV. According to Lenzer, the reasons provided for giving the vaccine to boys—gender equity and the prevention of oral and anal cancers—are not backed up by science. Lenzer also questions the HPV vaccine's effectiveness in preventing cancer in women and believes marketing and money may have something to do with the push to vaccinate boys.

Lenzer is a medical investigative journalist and frequent contributor to the *British Medical Journal.* Her work has been published in the *Atlantic,* the *New York Times Magazine, Newsweek Japan*, and many other outlets.

Merck's promotion of Gardasil, its vaccine against the human papilloma virus (HPV), has a complicated history. First there was the exuberant claim about its reputedly great effectiveness in preventing cervical cancer. Now comes the recommendation last month [October 2011] from the Centers for Disease Control and Prevention [CDC], that all 11- and 12-year-old boys should be given the vaccine.

Taking a Closer Look at Effectiveness Claims

The vaccine for boys is important, say advocates, because reducing HPV in boys will reduce transmission to girls and women—only 32 percent of whom have been getting the shots to date. Giving the shots to boys, they say, promotes gender equity. As a bonus, the vaccine may protect against oral and anal cancers in men who have sex with men.

Since a key part of the rationale for vaccinating boys is to protect girls, it's worth a moment to examine the claims about reducing cervical cancer deaths. Merck won approval for Gardasil from the Food and Drug Administration [FDA] in June 2006. On May 10, 2007, Merck published the results of a study in the *New England Journal of Medicine* that claimed an astounding 98 percent efficacy in preventing changes in the cervix used as a *marker* for cervical cancer.

But that statistic begs closer examination.

To achieve the 98 percent efficacy claim, Merck excluded from analysis anyone who "violated" the study protocol. In other words, all real-world problems that arose were excluded from analysis. Problems like girls who refused to take a second or third shot after they became sick and (correctly or incorrectly) blamed the vaccine. Or doctors who incorrectly gave the vaccine to someone who shouldn't have received it. While it's worth knowing how effective the vaccine is when it's used exactly as it should be, for a public-health decision, it's not as relevant as its real-world effectiveness.

To Merck's credit, they reported that when *all* women in the study were analyzed, the vaccine's efficacy dropped to 44 percent. Still, 44 percent might be considered a smashing success when you're talking about saving lives.

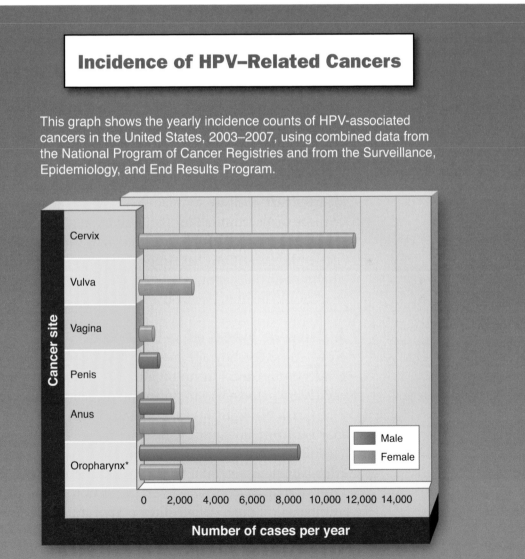

Incidence of HPV–Related Cancers

This graph shows the yearly incidence counts of HPV-associated cancers in the United States, 2003–2007, using combined data from the National Program of Cancer Registries and from the Surveillance, Epidemiology, and End Results Program.

*The part of the throat at the back of the mouth.

Taken from: US Centers for Disease Control and Prevention. "Human Papillomavirus (HPV)–Associated Cancers."

Except for one thing: the numbers get worse. The 44 percent benefit included only those women with the two specific cancer-causing HPV strains found in the vaccine.

But when the researchers looked at negative cervical changes from any causes, they found that changes occurred in unvaccinated women at a rate of 1.5 events per 100 person-years, while vaccinated women had 1.3 events—dropping the benefit to 17 percent.

Moreover, most of the cervical changes tracked by the researchers weren't even indicative of cervical cancer in the first place. Most were innocent cellular abnormalities that either disappear entirely on their own, or never progress to cancer. In fact, when they looked more closely at advanced cervical changes most likely to progress to cancer versus more innocent changes that go away spontaneously, it was the innocent changes that accounted for the decline.

Whether Gardasil will reduce cervical cancer deaths in real-world conditions has simply never been answered. It might—but that would take a long-term study, and one that should be done *before* it's widely promoted.

A Cure in Need of a Disease

Now, come the boys. If cervical cancer prevention and gender equity don't have you jumping out of your seat to grab every preteen boy to get a shot, what about the claim that Gardasil might prevent anal and oral cancers men may get from having sex with other men?

Merck says that in males, the vaccine is 89 percent effective against genital warts and 75 percent effective against anal cancer. On closer inspection, some of the numbers don't just deflate, they evaporate. First off, let's define the problem: The annual number of deaths from anal-rectal cancer among all men in the U.S. is 300. And how did Merck get its happy statistics on efficacy? Once again, they reported an idealized benefit by excluding from analysis 1,250 study violators out of 4,055 total test subjects. When the real-world analysis was conducted, the numbers plunged—right down to plum nothing. After evaluating tissue changes in male genitalia that were suggestive of a cancer precursor, Merck reported that vaccine efficacy against such lesions "was not observed."

Given this, is it worth the risk of exposing millions of youth to the as yet uncertain harms of the vaccine? The CDC states that in rare instances, some vaccines may trigger the potentially fatal and paralyzing condition Guillain-Barré, and Nizar Souayah, MD, of the University of Medicine and Dentistry of New Jersey in Newark, says he and his colleagues found "clear evidence from our database of an increased incidence of Guillain-Barré syndrome in the first six weeks, especially the first two weeks, after [HPV] vaccination." Guillain-Barré is very rare, even among people who are HPV vaccinated, but the problem is emblematic of the downsides of subjecting millions of people to any medical treatment.

Financial Motivation

So how did the HPV vaccine become a multi-billion-dollar winner for Merck? Well you might not be surprised to hear that the company happily lavished money on doctors, professional societies, and over 100 legislators. Of course, there is no tie between the recipients of this largesse and their promotion of the vaccine, say beneficiaries like presidential candidate and current Texas governor Rick Perry. In 2007, Perry signed an executive decree mandating that all girls in Texas receive the vaccine. The $28,500 Perry received was minor compared to his other connection to Merck: Perry's chief of staff, Mike Toomey, became a lobbyist for Merck, championing the HPV vaccine. Once in that position, [he] announced his plans to raise over $50 million for Perry's presidential campaign.

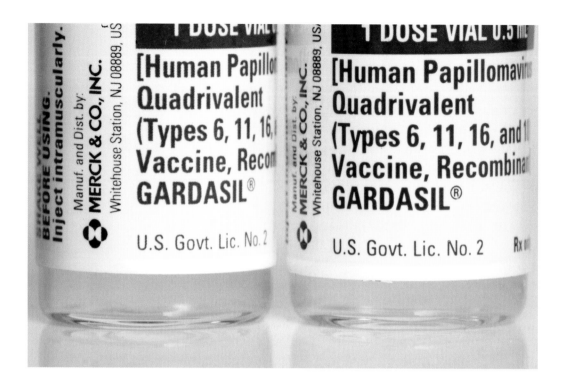

In an effort to promote the use of its HPV vaccine (shown), pharmaceutical giant Merck lavished money on doctors, professional societies, and over a hundred legislators, the author claims. (© Jb Reed/ Bloomberg via Getty Images)

In any case, the marketing certainly doesn't seem to have hurt the adoption of Gardasil, which has been administered to millions of girls around the country. Caught up in the joy, some 41 state legislatures have initiated bills to promote or mandate the shots for all girls. With the CDC's new recommendation for boys, one can imagine that promotion or mandates for them might come next.

Fortunately, some researchers don't believe the hype. Dr. Diane Harper, one of the lead researchers in the development of the HPV vaccine, recently told the *Kansas City Star*, the vaccine for boys is "pie in the sky. . . . We're short of health care dollars. Why should we spend it on that?"

Indeed. There are better ways to spend the billions of dollars currently being spent on HPV vaccines. First, we already have a pretty terrific way to prevent most cervical cancer deaths, and it's called the Pap smear. Since poor women are less likely to get Pap smears and more likely to die from cervical cancer, we could start by extending medical services to them. Second, many oral cancers are caused by smoking, and men and women who smoke are more likely to die of oral and cervical cancer, so we could invest in smoking cessation efforts.

As Angela Raffle, a specialist in cervical cancer screening, told the *New York Times'* Elisabeth Rosenthal, "Oh, dear. If we give it to boys, then all pretense of scientific worth and cost analysis goes out the window."

Unfortunately, the hope that we would undertake low-tech, high-yield public health efforts might be the real pie in the sky thinking.

The HPV Vaccine May Make Teens More Promiscuous

John F. Brehany and Maricela P. Moffitt

In the following viewpoint John F. Brehany and Maricela P. Moffit contend that the HPV vaccine might promote risky sexual behavior in teens. Brehany and Moffit think there may be reasons to give the vaccine to girls, but they are against giving it to boys. They worry that vaccinating homosexual boys will cause them to "feel protected" and embolden them to undertake risky sexual behavior. They express concern that this behavior may occur in vaccinated girls, as well.

Brehany is the executive director and Maricela P. Moffitt is president of the Catholic Medical Association.

O n Oct. 25, 2011, the Advisory Committee on Immunization Practices (ACIP) recommended that all 11- and 12-year-old boys be routinely vaccinated against human papillomavirus (HPV). This questionable decision should make Catholics re-examine

SOURCE: John F. Brehany and Maricela P. Moffitt, "Immunization of Boys Against HPV: Neither Sound Ethics Nor Sound Public Policy," *National Catholic Register,* October 25, 2011. http://www.nc register.com. Copyright © 2011 by the National Catholic Register. All rights reserved. Reproduced by permission.

the issue of HPV immunization and redouble their efforts to build a culture of life, particularly in matters of health and health care. A little history is in order to put this decision into proper context.

In June 2006, the ACIP recommended routine immunization of girls against HPV to reduce rates of cervical cancer among women. About 12,000 women in the U.S. get cervical cancer each year, and HPV, a sexually transmitted disease (STD), is the main cause of cervical cancer.

HPV Vaccination May Be Acceptable for Girls

There are several reasons why the Catholic Medical Association (CMA) has recognized that immunizing girls against HPV can be an acceptable public-health policy and an ethical option that individuals or parents may choose.

In reputable clinical trials, Merck's Gardasil and GlaxoSmithKline's Cervarix have been shown to be safe and effective at protecting against some three to five strains of HPV, respectively (out of more than 40 total genital strains), which cause most cervical cancer. Both drugs are expensive, at about $130/dose, with three doses recommended for complete protection.

Still, cost-effectiveness models have estimated that a program of universal vaccination of adolescent girls will cost $23,000–$45,000 per quality-adjusted life year (QALY) saved, which falls within a range generally deemed acceptable for preventive medicine.

HPV immunization can be an ethical option for individuals and parents to choose. Of course, no one should choose a means of protection in order to purposely facilitate immoral action. But the Church does not demand that individuals be made to suffer the full effects of their bad judgments. And healing and preventing diseases, no matter what their source, are acts of mercy.

A teenager gets an HPV vaccine injection. Many religious groups think vaccinating girls against HPV will make them sexually promiscuous. (© Helene Rogers/Art Directors & TRIP/Alamy)

While it is possible to screen for and treat cervical cancer without immunization, such interventions bring their own burdens. False-positive results during cancer screening cause significant emotional distress for an individual and a couple. And surgically removing precancerous lesions can cause increased rates of both preterm deliveries and cesarean-section deliveries.

However, even with the most generous interpretation of the public-health policy and ethical analysis, significant questions remain. For example:

- What is the long-term effectiveness of HPV immunization? No studies have yet been published on whether the vaccines confer immunity for an extended period, e.g., 15-plus years. Moreover, it is still not certain whether HPV immunity in the teenage years will truly reduce cancer rates 20–40 years later, when most cervical cancer develops.

- What is the real (not theoretical) cost-effectiveness of HPV immunization? Current cost-benefit ratios are based on 70%–75% of all girls being fully immunized. But less than 50% of girls have received even one dose of vaccine; only 33% have received all three.
- Will there be negative behavioral responses to the immunization campaign? If immunized girls improperly feel "protected"—engaging in more risky, immoral behaviors and failing to consistently receive annual pap smears—then HPV immunization will fail to deliver the hoped-for benefits.

Even if a case can be made for the routine immunization of girls (while always respecting the free and informed consent of parents and individuals), the same case cannot be made for boys.

Key Differences of Vaccinating Girls and Boys

ACIP officials attempted to put the best spin on their decision—appealing to the goals of preventing more cancers, "gender equity" and adding a layer of protection for girls. But key differences exist in terms of public-health goals and cost-benefit analysis.

For starters, while Gardasil can prevent some precursors to cancer resulting from male homosexual activity, these cancers are less common and generally more treatable than cervical cancer in women. Because of this, and because the marginal benefit to girls of immunizing boys is relatively limited, the cost of prevention would rise from $23,000–45,000 to hundreds of thousands of dollars per QALY. This makes no sense in terms of sound public policy. Nor is it in the best interests of one of the ACIP's target populations—boys engaged in homosexual acts.

If immunized boys feel protected, and engage in more risky, immoral behavior, while seeking less medical

> **FAST FACT**
>
> Gay and bisexual men are about seventeen times more likely to develop anal cancer than men who only have sex with women, according to the US Centers for Disease Control and Prevention.

The Prevalence of Genital Warts

This graph shows the prevalence of genital warts among sexually transmitted disease (STD) clinic patients by sex, sex of partners, and site, 2010.

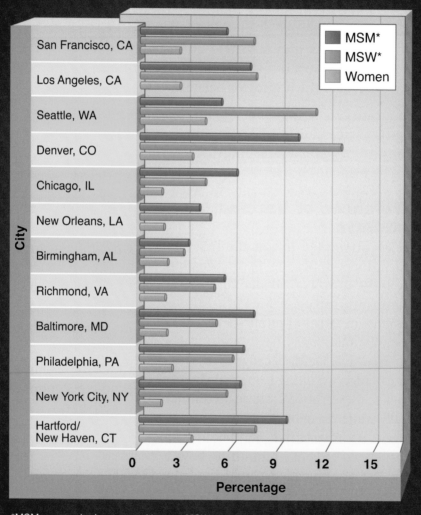

*MSM = men who have sex with men; MSW = men who have sex with women only.

Taken from: US Centers for Disease Control and Prevention STD Surveillance Network.

attention, the consequences for their physical and moral health will be devastating.

The ACIP's questionable decision illustrates some key individual and institutional failings that are bringing our nation to a point of crisis. On the one hand, the promiscuous sexual behavior of many individuals is creating an epidemic of STDs, including the symptomless disease of HPV, which causes cancer years after it has been contracted.

On the other hand, a technophilic approach to medicine, combined with a big-government approach to spending and intervening in family matters, will create an expensive, bureaucratic solution of questionable prudence to a problem that can be better met through formation in the virtues.

Ideally, the ethical evaluation of HPV immunization should be conducted in terms of reliable data and moral prudence, yet the real world of American health care and public policy is charged with a variety of agents and agendas.

For example, the ACIP recommended routine immunization of girls in June 2006, even though the first phase-3 trials of the HPV vaccine with clinically relevant end points weren't reported until May 2007.

From the start, Merck engaged in a political full-court press to persuade states to mandate HPV immunization. And, as the Catholics for the Common Good has revealed, Merck has given hundreds of thousands of dollars to medical societies like the American College of Obstetricians and Gynecologists to help persuade key decision-makers to encourage HPV immunization.

Most recently, these efforts culminated in a new law in California that permits children as young as 12 years old to accept HPV immunization without parental consent.

Catholics should not recuse themselves from this debate. They should be engaged both in challenging the secular solutions that are being put forward and in creating alternatives that better protect human health and human life.

The HPV Vaccine Does Not Promote Teen Promiscuity

Christopher Wanjek

In the following viewpoint Christopher Wanjek contends that vaccinating young girls against HPV does not make them more promiscuous. According to Wanjek, a study conducted by the US Centers for Disease Control and Prevention found no difference in the sexual activity of young women who did and who did not receive the HPV vaccine. Wanjek is not surprised by the study; vaccines in general do not encourage risky behavior, he says.

Wanjek is the author of the books *Bad Medicine* and *Food at Work*. His column, Bad Medicine, appears regularly on the science news website LiveScience.

Young women who receive the vaccine for the human papillomavirus (HPV) are no more likely to engage in sex or risky sexual behavior than women the same age not vaccinated, according to a CDC [US Centers for Disease Control and Prevention] study [appearing] in the January [2012] issue of the *American Journal of Preventive Medicine.*

Few in the public health community are surprised by the results, however. Vaccines simply aren't known to encourage risky behavior. Why should the HPV vaccine be different?

That is, people who get the flu shot are no more inclined to rub their eyeballs into a doorknob than people who don't get the flu shot. People who get a tetanus shot are no more inclined to purposely puncture themselves with a rusty nail from the boardwalk of Coney Island

A Centers for Disease Control and Prevention study found the use of HPV vaccine in girls aged fifteen to twenty-four made them no more likely to engage in sexually promiscuous behavior than those not receiving the vaccine. (© Chris Rout/Alamy)

than those who don't get a tetanus shot. And so on with every vaccine and every route of exposure.

Concerns Stem from the Way HPV Is Transmitted

HPV is the most common sexually transmitted disease in the United States, with an estimated 6.2 million new infections annually, according to the study. HPV infection causes over 90 percent of cervical cancer cases, and most women will have at least one strain of the virus by the time they are 50, according to the CDC. The virus kills a quarter-million women annually, mostly in poor countries.

Sounds dangerous. You'd think the HPV vaccine would have been treated as a godsend. Instead, the vaccine, sold in the United States under the names Gardasil and Cervarix, has met nothing but controversy.

The issue is that the prime recipients of the HPV vaccine are girls, preferably virgins. The worry in some circles is that the HPV vaccine offers an excuse for them to start fooling around.

That is, maybe young women would become sexually active once they were protected from HPV—a virus they never heard of, which can cause cancer in another 20-some years should they fail to see a gynecologist for a pap smear— because surely they'd think that this vaccine also would protect them from all the things they *have* heard about: pregnancy, HIV, syphilis, gonorrhea, genital herpes and pubic lice.

Note that girls aren't any more inclined to be sexually active after receiving the hepatitis B vaccine as an infant to prevent that sexually transmitted disease; but still, there's been worry.

FAST FACT

HPV can occur as a coinfection with another virus. According to the International Agency for Research on Cancer, HIV and chlamydia are the coinfections that are most consistently reported to have an epidemiological association with persistent HPV infection and cervical cancer.

Many Who Opted Out of the HPV Vaccine Felt They Were Not at Risk

Among the girls and women surveyed who did not receive the HPV vaccine, the primary reason given for opting out was that they felt they were not at risk of contracting HPV; 1,243 girls and women aged 15–24 were surveyed in the National Survey of Family Growth in 2007–2008.

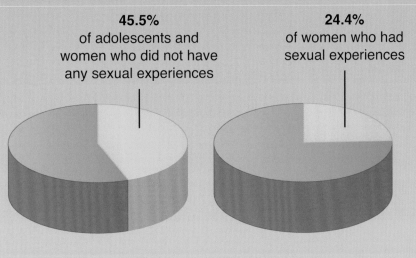

45.5%
of adolescents and women who did not have any sexual experiences

24.4%
of women who had sexual experiences

Taken from: N.C. Liddon, J.E. Hood, and J.S. Leichliter. "Intent to Receive HPV Vaccine and Reasons for Not Vaccinating Among Unvaccinated Adolescent and Young Women: Findings from the 2006–2008 National Survey of Family Growth." *Vaccine*, March 2012.

No Increase in Promiscuity

The CDC study is based on a survey of 1,243 young women ages 15 to 24, interviewed as part of the National Survey of Family Growth. The researchers found that those who received the HPV vaccine were no more likely to have begun having sex before age 15 or to have had more sexual partners compared with those who didn't get the vaccine.

In fact, sexually active women who had received the vaccine were more likely to use condoms. The authors attributed this to the fact that the women were more knowledgeable about the dangers of sexually transmitted diseases.

The CDC study likely won't appease the HPV vaccine's many adversaries. But it might give state governments more courage to make the vaccine mandatory for boys and girls.

And once we get vaccines to prevent HIV, syphilis, gonorrhea, genital herpes and pubic lice, then we can start worrying about promiscuity.

Abstinence-Only Programs Are the Best Way to Prevent Disease and Other Problems

American College of Pediatricians

In the following viewpoint the American College of Pediatricians (ACPeds) argues that abstinence-until-marriage sex education programs are the most effective way to protect adolescents from getting HPV or other sexually transmitted infections (STIs). The ACPeds believes programs that promote abstinence until marriage are better than comprehensive sex education at reducing adolescent sexual activity. Focusing on contraception, as sex education programs do, reinforces the message that sexual activity is OK, says the ACPeds, and this is not the message adolescents need to hear. According to the ACPeds, adolescents need clear guidance about the dangers of sexual activity, such as the risk of contracting HPV.

ACPeds is a national organization of socially conservative pediatricians and other health care professionals that split from the American Academy of Pediatrics over the latter's support for gay adoption. In a position statement at its website, the organization describes as "unhealthy and ill-advised" all sexual activity "outside of a monogamous, heterosexual, married relationship."

SOURCE: "Abstinence Education," American College of Pediatricians, October 2010. http://www.acpeds.org. Copyright © 2010 by the American College of Pediatricians. All rights reserved. Reproduced by permission.

The American College of Pediatricians strongly endorses abstinence-until-marriage sex education and recommends adoption by all school systems in lieu of "comprehensive sex education". This position is based on [what L.P. Freedman describes as] "the public health principle of primary prevention—risk avoidance in lieu of risk reduction," upholding the "human right to the highest attainable standard of health."

Sexually Active Adolescents Face Significant Risks

By every measure, adolescent sexual activity is detrimental to the well-being of all involved, especially young women, and society at large. Children and adolescents from 10 to 19 years of age are more at risk for contracting a sexually transmitted infection (STI) than adults. This is due to the general practice of having multiple and higher risk sexual partners, and to the immaturity of the cervical tissue of girls and young women. The CDC [US Centers for Disease Control and Prevention] recently stated that of the 19 million new cases of STIs annually reported in the United States, 50 percent occur in teens and young adults under 25 years of age. Twenty-five percent of newly diagnosed cases of HIV occur in those under 22 years of age. This translates into one in four sexually active female adolescents being infected with at least one STI.

Bacterial STIs may cause life-threatening cases of pelvic inflammatory disease (PID) and infertility. Viral STIs which include herpes, the Human Papilloma Virus (HPV) and HIV are generally incurable. Herpes afflicts its victims with life-long painful recurrences, may be passed on to sexual partners even when asymptomatic, and may be life threatening to infants if passed on at birth during vaginal delivery. HPV is found among 90 percent of sexually active young adults and teens. While often self-limited, HPV has high-risk strains that may persist for life and cause cancer of the cervix. HIV not only causes premature demise, but also significant suffering with life-long dependence on multiple toxic and costly medications. The CDC estimates that STIs cost the U.S. health care system as much as $15.3 billion annually.

Adolescent pregnancy is similarly associated with adverse socioeconomics that have an impact on the family, community, and society at large. One in thirteen high school girls becomes pregnant each year. Adolescent pregnancy results in decreased educational and vocational opportunities for the mothers, an increased likelihood of the family living in poverty, and significant risk for negative long-term outcomes for the children. For example, children of adolescent mothers are more likely to be born prematurely and at a low birth weight; suffer from poor health; perform poorly in school; run away from home; be abused or neglected; and grow up without a father.

Even if sexually active teens escape acquiring sexually transmitted infections (STIs) and becoming pregnant, few remain emotionally unscathed. Overall, one in eight teens suffers from depression, and suicide has risen to become the third leading cause of death for adolescents, paralleling the rise in STIs within this population. Infection with an STI has long been recognized as a cause for depression among teens. More recently, however, adolescent sexual activity alone has been acknowledged as an independent risk factor for developing low self-esteem, major depression, and attempting suicide. In studies that controlled for confounding factors, sexually active girls were found to be three times as likely to report being depressed and three times as likely to have attempted suicide when compared to sexually abstinent girls. Sexually active boys were more than twice as likely to suffer from depression and seven times as likely to have attempted suicide when compared to sexually abstinent boys. This is not mere coincidence. Scientists now know that sexual activity releases chemicals in the brain that create emotional bonds between partners. Breaking these bonds can cause depression, and make it harder to bond with someone else in the future.

Abstinence Versus Sex Education Programs

Sexual activity is defined as genital contact. This includes mutual masturbation, as well as oral, vaginal, and anal intercourse. While only vaginal intercourse may result in pregnancy, all of these practices may spread STIs, and lead to emotional trauma. Abstaining from all sexual activity is the only 100 percent safe and effective way to avoid teen pregnancies, STIs, and the emotional fallout of adolescent sexual activity. Almost 40 years of emphasis on "safer sex" with "values-neutral sex education," condoms and contraception has clearly failed our young people. Abstinence education does not occur in a vacuum, making it especially difficult to separate its influence from the opposing influence of the media and cultural milieu. Nevertheless, effectiveness of abstinence sex education in delaying the onset of sexual debut has been demonstrated in rigorous scientific studies. For example, five out of seven programs recently reviewed showed a significant reduction in sexual initiation rates (two programs showed rates decreased by half). Evaluation of community-based abstinence programs in peer-reviewed journals showed that they are effective in significantly reducing pregnancy. According to an April 2008 report by the Heritage Foundation "fifteen studies examined abstinence programs and eleven reported positive findings of delayed sexual initiation." Reviews by The Institute for Research and Evaluation state that "several well designed evaluations of abstinence programs have found significant long-term reductions in adolescent sexual activity." These do not begin to thoroughly evaluate the hundreds of ongoing programs.

In its endorsement of abstinence-based sex education, the College calls attention to the scientific controversies

Content Requirements for Sex Education

When provided, sex education* must include information on:

State	Contraception	Abstinence	Importance of Sex Only Within Marriage	Sexual Orientation	Negative Outcomes of Teen Sex
Alabama	X	Stress	X	Negative	X
Arizona		Stress			X
Arkansas		Stress	X		
California	X	Cover		Inclusive	
Colorado	X	Stress			
Delaware	X	Stress		Inclusive	
District of Columbia	X				
Florida		Stress	X		X
Georgia		Stress	X		X
Hawaii	X	Cover			
Illinois		Stress	X		X
Indiana		Stress	X		
Iowa				Inclusive	
Kentucky		Cover			X
Louisiana		Stress	X		
Maine	X	Stress			
Maryland	X	Cover			
Michigan		Stress	X		X
Minnesota		Cover			
Mississippi**	**	Stress	X		X
Missouri		Stress	X		X
Montana		Cover			
New Hampshire					
New Jersey	X	Stress		Inclusive	
New Mexico	X	Cover		Inclusive	
New York					
North Carolina	X	Stress	X		
North Dakota		Cover			
Ohio		Stress	X		X
Oklahoma		Stress			
Oregon	X	Stress		Inclusive	
Pennsylvania					
Rhode Island	X	Stress		Inclusive	
South Carolina	X	Stress	X	Negative	
Tennessee		Stress	X		X
Texas		Stress	X	Negative	X
Utah***		Stress	X		
Vermont	X	Cover			
Virginia	X	Cover	X		
Washington	X	Stress		Washington	
West Virginia	X	Cover	X		X
Wisconsin		Stress	X		
TOTAL	**17+DC**		**19**	**11**	**13**

* Sex education typically includes discussion of sexually transmitted infections (STIs).
** Localities may omit state-required topics, but may not include material that "contradicts the required components." Information on contraception may only be provided with prior approval from the Department of Education.
*** State also prohibits teachers from responding to students' spontaneous questions in ways that conflict with the law's requirements.

Taken from: Guttmacher Institute. "Sex and HIV Education," May 1, 2012. www.guttmacher.org/statecenter/spibs/spib_SE.pdf.

surrounding alternative educational platforms. Most sex education curricula fall into two categories, *abstinence-until-marriage* or *comprehensive sex education programs* (occasionally also referred to as "abstinence plus" programs). Recently, abstinence education has been criticized for not providing critical health information about condom use. Abstinence education curricula, however, do not discourage the use of condoms; rather they note that chastity obviates the need for condoms. Abstinence education programs do not claim that condoms have no place in preventing STIs. Comprehensive programs, on the other hand, are misleading in the emphasis they place on condom use. These programs give teens the impression that condoms make sexual activity safe. In reality, there has been much conflicting medical literature on the effectiveness of condoms in preventing STIs since the 2000 NIH [National Institutes of Health] report on the subject and much of the controversy remains unresolved. Teens must be informed that condoms do not offer complete protection from either pregnancy or STIs.

FAST FACT

According to the National Immunization Survey for Teens, in 2010 approximately 48.7 percent of adolescents aged thirteen to seventeen had received at least one shot of the recommended three-dose HPV vaccine.

The College position supporting abstinence-until-marriage education, unlike alternative education platforms, also recognizes the unique neurobiology of adolescent brains. The frontal cortex of the adolescent brain is still in development and unable to make the consistently wise executive decisions necessary to control action based on emotional input. Researcher Jay Giedd and others have found that young people do not have the physical brain capacity to make fully mature decisions until their mid-twenties.

Consequently, when it comes to sex education, adolescents need to be given clear direction repeatedly, as is done with programs that address smoking, drugs, and alcohol use. Emphasis on contraceptive methods undermines the authority of parents and the strength of the abstinence message. This approach reinforces the ubiquitous (yet erroneous) message presented by the media that engaging in sexual activity is not only expected of teens, but also the norm. Adolescent brains are not equipped to handle these mixed messages. Parents and teachers need to "function as a surrogate set of frontal lobes, an auxiliary problem solver" for their teens, setting firm and immutable expectations. Adolescents need repetitive, clear, and consistent guidance.

The Importance of Parental Involvement

As families address this issue of sex education, the American College of Pediatricians recommends that parents be fully aware of the content of the curriculum to which their children are being exposed. The national "Guidelines for Comprehensive Sex Education" that were drafted by the Sexuality Information and Education Council of the United States (SIECUS) place strong emphasis on "values neutral" sex education beginning in *kindergarten*. According to these guidelines, children between the ages of 5 to 8 should be taught not only the anatomically correct names of all body parts, but also the definitions of sexual intercourse, and masturbation.

Overall, these comprehensive programs only emphasize "safer sex." Many comprehensive programs also provide sexually erotic material to teens with explicit condom demonstrations. Other programs suggest alternative types of sexually stimulating contact (referred to as "outercourse") that would not result in pregnancy but still could result in STIs. Some of these activities, depending on the ages of those involved and the state in which they occur, could actually be illegal. These education programs can break down the natural barriers of those not yet involved in sexual activity and encourage experimentation. Additionally, many programs emphasize that teens do not need parental consent to obtain birth control and that teens therefore need not even discuss the issue with them.

Discouraging parental involvement eliminates one of the most powerful deterrents to sexual activity, namely, communication of parental expectations. Firm statements from parents that sex should be reserved for marriage have been found to be very effective in delaying sexual debut. Parental example and "religiosity" have also been found to be similarly protective. Adolescents reared by parents who live according to their professed faith and are actively involved in their worship community, are more likely to abstain from sexual activity as teens. Successful sex education programs involve parents and promote open discussion between parents and their children.

The American College of Pediatricians also believes parents should be aware of the current state of funding, and government involvement in sex education choices. Comprehensive programs receive seven to twelve times the funding of abstinence programs. However, according to a recent study by the Department of Health and Human Services, comprehensive programs do not give equal time to abstinence.

In 2004 Congressman Henry Waxman of California presented a report before Congress critical of the medical accuracy of abstinence education curricula. The Mathematica Study was similarly critical of the medical accuracy of abstinence education programs. However, in 2007 the U.S. Department of Health and Human Services [HHS] conducted an extensive review of nine comprehensive sex education curricula using the same methods employed by Congressman Waxman and the Mathematica Study. These comprehensive programs were found to have no better record for medical accuracy. The HHS review also found that the comprehensive programs were hardly comprehensive. The amount of discussion dedicated to "safer sex" exceeded that spent on abstinence by

a factor of up to seven. Some of the programs failed to mention abstinence altogether. None of the programs carefully distinguished between reducing and eliminating the risks of sexual activity, and nearly every program failed to mention the emotional consequences of early sexual activity. Although some of the comprehensive programs showed a small effect in reducing "unprotected" sex (7 of 9 programs) and to a lesser extent in delaying sexual debut (2 of 8 programs), the impact did not extend beyond six months.

According to a 2004 Zogby Poll, 90% of adults and teens agree with The American College of Pediatricians position that teens should be given a strong abstinence messaged. Programs that teach sexual abstinence until marriage are about much more than simply delaying sexual activity. They assist adolescents in establishing positive character traits, formulating long-term goals, and developing emotionally healthy relationships. These programs increase the likelihood of strong marriages and families—the single most essential resource for the strength and survival of our nation.

A sex education teacher talks to students about sex. Many experts believe knowing about sex helps young people avoid disease better than promoting abstinence does. (© AP Images/Alan Diaz)

Abstinence-Only Programs Are Ineffective at Preventing Disease and Other Problems

Advocates for Youth

In the following viewpoint Advocates for Youth (AFY) contends that the best way to reduce HPV and other sexually transmitted infections (STIs) is by providing adolescents with accurate, balanced sex education, including information about contraception and condom use. According to AFY, abstinence programs underemphasize the effectiveness of condoms, even suggesting that condoms do not protect against HPV—one of many myths abstinence program proponents disseminate.

AFY is a nonprofit organization that works to help young people in the United States and in developing countries make informed and responsible decisions about their reproductive and sexual health.

Accurate, balanced sex education—including information about contraception and condoms—is a basic human right of youth. Such education helps young people to reduce their risk of potentially negative outcomes, such as unwanted pregnancies and sexually transmitted infections (STIs). Such education can also help youth to enhance the quality of their relationships and to develop decision-making skills that will prove invaluable over life. This basic human right is also a core public health principle that receives strong endorsement from mainstream medical associations, public health and educational organizations, and—most important—parents.

Yet, federal policy makers have provided large amounts of funding for abstinence-only education—programs that ignore youth's basic human right and the fundamental public health principle of accurate, balanced sex education. Abstinence-only programs are geared to prevent teens—and sometimes all unmarried people—from engaging in any sexual activity. Indeed, the federal government has gone so far as to specify that these programs must have, as their "exclusive purpose," the promotion of abstinence outside of marriage and that they must not, in any way, advocate contraceptive use or discuss contraceptive methods, other than to emphasize their failure rates. Since 1998, over $1.5 billion in state and federal funds has been allocated for these abstinence-only and abstinence-only-until-marriage (hereafter collectively referred to as abstinence-only) education programs.

This document explores some of the claims that have been put forward to support federal funding for abstinence-only education rather than for comprehensive sex education.

The Claim: Research shows that abstinence-only education delays sexual initiation and reduces teen pregnancy.

The Facts: Abstinence-only education programs are not effective at delaying the initiation of sexual activity or in reducing teen pregnancy.

- A long-awaited, federally-funded evaluation of four carefully selected abstinence-only education programs, published in April 2007, showed that youth enrolled in the programs were no more likely than those not in the programs to delay sexual initiation, to have fewer sexual partners, or to abstain entirely from sex.

• Numerous state evaluations of federally-funded programs have yielded similar conclusions. A 2004 review by Advocates for Youth of 11 state-based evaluations found that abstinence-only programs showed little evidence of sustained (long-term) impact on attitudes and intentions. Worse, they showed some negative impacts on youth's willingness to use contraception, including condoms, to prevent negative sexual health outcomes related to sexual intercourse. In only one state did any program demonstrate *short*-term success in youth's delaying the initiation of sex. *None* of the programs showed evidence of *long*-term success in delaying sexual initiation among youth enrolled in the programs. *None* of the programs showed any evidence of success in reducing other sexual risk-taking behaviors among participants. More specifically, a 2003 Pennsylvania evaluation found that the state-sponsored programs were largely ineffective in delaying sexual onset or promoting skills and attitudes consistent with sexual abstinence. Arizona and Kansas had similar findings of no change in behaviors. A 2004 evaluation from Texas found no significant changes in the percentage of students who pledged not to have sex until marriage. As in two other studies, the Texas analysis revealed that the percentage of students who reported having engaged in sexual intercourse increased for nearly all ages.

• Robert Rector of the Heritage Foundation claimed that many studies showed that abstinence programs *were* effective in reducing youth's sexual activity. However, in a 2002 review of the ten studies cited by Rector, Douglas Kirby PhD, a widely recognized, highly reputable evaluator of sex education programs for youth, concluded that nine failed to provide credible evidence, consistent with accepted standards of research, that they delayed the initiation of sex or reduced the frequency of sex. One study provided some evidence that the program *may* have delayed the initiation of sex among youth 15 and younger but not among those 17 and younger.

The Claim: Abstinence-only programs are responsible for the recent dramatic decline in teen pregnancy.

The Facts: A new study showed that improved contraceptive use is responsible for 86 percent of the decline in the U.S. adolescent pregnancy rate between 1995 and 2002. Dramatic improvements in contraceptive use, including increases in the use of single methods, increases in the use of multiple methods, and declines in nonuse are responsible for improved adolescent pregnancy rates. Only 14 percent of the change among 15- to 19-year-olds

A "virginity pledge" ceremony, during which teens promise to remain virgins until marriage, is pictured. Many religious groups maintain that abstinence is the best way for teens to avoid diseases like HPV. (© **Marvi Lacar/Getty Images**)

was attributable to a decrease in the percentage of sexually active young women.

Even though the teen birth rate in 2005 fell to 40.4 births per 1,000 women ages 15 through 19, the lowest rate in 65 years, the United States continues to have the highest teen birth rate of any of the world's developed nations. Almost 750,000 teenage women become pregnant in the United States each year. Nearly three in 10 U.S. teenage women experience pregnancy. The U.S. teen birth rate is one and a half times higher than that in the United Kingdom and more than twice as high as that in Canada.

The Claim: Virginity pledges (public promises to remain a virgin until marriage), a common component of abstinence-only programs, delay the onset of sexual activity and protect teens from STIs.

The Facts: Research suggests that, under certain very limited conditions, pledging may help *some* adolescents to delay sexual intercourse. One study found that the onset of sexual activity was delayed 18 months among pledgers; however, the study also found that those young people who took a pledge were one-third less likely than their non-pledging peers to use contraception when they did become sexually active. In addition, although pledgers were consistently less likely to be exposed to risk factors across a wide range of indicators, their rate of sexually transmitted infections (STIs) did not differ from non-pledgers, possibly because they were less likely to use condoms at sexual debut. They were also less likely to seek STI testing and diagnosis.

Virginity pledges are particularly problematic for teens that have been sexually assaulted or sexually abused and for teens who are gay and lesbian. In addition, many see virginity pledging as a faith-based message pretending to be a secular, public health message.

The Claim: Abstinence-only-until-marriage programs reflect American values.

The Facts: Objective data confirm that abstinence-until-marriage does not reflect American values. The median age of sexual initiation among Americans is 17 and the average age of marriage is 25.8 for women and 27.4 for men. This age difference clearly indicates a long time between sexual onset and marriage. In a major, nationally representative survey, 95 percent of adult respondents, ages 18 through 44, reported that they had sex before marriage. Even among those who abstained from sex until age 20 or older, 81 percent reported having had premarital sex.

The Claim: Abstinence-only programs provide accurate, unbiased information about reproductive health.

The Facts: Many of the curricula commonly used in abstinence-only programs distort information about the effectiveness of contraceptives, misrepresent the risks of abortion, blur religion and science, treat gender stereotypes as scientific fact, and contain basic scientific errors, according to a 2004 report by Government Reform Committee staff. The report reviewed the 13 most commonly used curricula and concluded that two of the curricula were accurate but that 11 others, used by 69 organizations in 25 states, contained unproven assertions, subjective conclusions, or outright falsehoods regarding reproductive health, gender traits, and when life begins. Among the distortions cited by Government Reform Committee staff: a 43-day-old fetus is a "thinking person"; HIV can be spread via sweat and tears; condoms fail to prevent HIV transmission as often as 31 percent of the time in heterosexual intercourse; women who have an abortion "are more prone to suicide"; and as many as 10 percent of women who have abortions become sterile.

The Claim: Parents want abstinence-only education to be taught in schools.

The Facts: Most Americans want far more than abstinence-only in schools. Only 15 percent of American adults believe that schools should teach abstinence from sexual intercourse and should not provide information on how to obtain and use condoms and other contraception.

Most Americans want a broad sex education curriculum that teaches the basics—from how babies are made to how to put on a condom and how to get tested for STIs.

- 99 percent want youth to get information on other STIs in addition to HIV.
- 98 percent want youth to be taught about HIV/AIDS.
- 96 percent want youth to learn the "basics of how babies are made."
- 94 percent want youth to learn how to get tested for HIV and other STIs.
- 93 percent want youth to be taught about "waiting to have sexual intercourse until married."
- 83 percent want youth to know how to put on a condom.
- 71 percent believe that teens need to know that they can "obtain birth control pills from family planning clinics without permission from a parent."

The Claim: For every $1 spent on abstinence-only programs, the federal government spends $12 on comprehensive sex ed programs.

The Facts: There is no dedicated federal funding stream for comprehensive sex ed programs. This faulty analysis pretends that federal funding for health services for low income women and adolescents is, instead, funding for comprehensive sex education. It is not.

Programs—including Medicaid and Title X of the Public Health Service Act—are not comprehensive sex education programs—or educational programs at all. Rather, Medicaid is the health insurance program for the poorest Americans; it pays providers for medical services, including family planning. Title X supports the delivery of a broad package of family planning and related health services to low-income adults and teens through a nationwide network of family planning clinics. Title X services include not only contraceptive methods, but also Pap smears, breast exams, screening and treatment for STIs, and screening for hypertension, diabetes, and anemia.

It is more appropriate to compare what the federal government spends on abstinence-only education with what it spends on more comprehensive educational efforts that include both abstinence and contraception. Only one federally funded effort comes even close to meeting this description. It is the HIV prevention efforts of the Centers for Disease Control & Prevention, Division of Adolescent and School Health (CDC-DASH). It is unclear how much of the CDC-DASH HIV prevention budget (approximately $48 million) actually goes to direct education that includes a discussion of both abstinence and risk-reduction (condom use, to be precise). But since the HIV prevention budget also supports a wide range of other activities, including large-scale surveillance research like the national Youth Risk Behavior Survey, it is evident that not a great deal goes to comprehensive HIV prevention education—certainly nowhere near as much as the abstinence-only funds.

FAST FACT

Consistent condom use cuts a woman's risk of infection with HPV by 70 percent, according to a University of Washington study published in the *New England Journal of Medicine* in 2006.

The Claim: Condoms have a high failure rate in preventing unintended pregnancy.

The Facts: When a couple uses condoms consistently and correctly at every act of vaginal intercourse, a woman's chance of becoming pregnant within one year is less than three percent. Because some couples that use condoms use them less than every time and/or use them incorrectly, the *average* risk of becoming pregnant within one year is 15 percent. By contrast, when couples use no

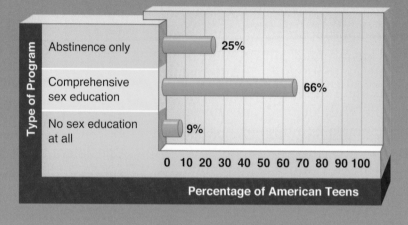

Most Teens Receive Comprehensive Sex Education

Those participating in comprehensive sex education programs were 60 percent less likely to get pregnant than those who received no sex education.

Type of Program

- Abstinence only — 25%
- Comprehensive sex education — 66%
- No sex education at all — 9%

0 10 20 30 40 50 60 70 80 90 100

Percentage of American Teens

Taken from: Pamela Kohler, Lisa Manhart, and William Lafferty. "Abstinence Only and Comprehensive Sex Education and the Initiation of Sexual Activity and Teen Pregnancy." *Journal of Adolescent Health*, April 2008.

protection, a woman has an 85 percent chance of becoming pregnant within one year.

The Claim: Condoms do not protect against human papillomavirus (HPV).

The Facts: When condoms are used correctly and consistently, they can help prevent the spread of HPV and can reduce the risk of HPV-associated diseases, such as cervical cancer and genital warts. However, since HPV is spread by skin-to-skin contact, infection can occur in areas that are not covered or protected by a condom. In 2001, a panel of experts convened by the National Institutes of Health (NIH) concluded that condom use can reduce the risk of HPV-associated disease. An HPV vaccine that can protect against the two strains responsible for 70 percent of cervical cancer was approved by the FDA [Food and Drug Administration] in 2006 and recommended by the CDC for young women ages 11 through 26. In addition, CDC recommended routine, annual Pap tests for sexually active young women, in order to achieve early detection of HPV-associated problems.

The Claim: Condoms are not effective in preventing the transmission of HIV and other STIs.

The Facts: Condoms are a highly effective public health tool in the fight against HIV infection. A study of HIV-serodiscordant couples in Europe (where one person is HIV-infected and his/her partner is not) found *no* HIV transmission to the uninfected partner among any of the 124 couples who used a condom at every act of sexual intercourse. Among those couples that were inconsistent users of condoms, 12 percent of the uninfected partners became infected with HIV. The 2001 report from NIH also confirmed that condoms are very effective in affording protection against HIV. An NIH review of laboratory studies showed that condoms afford good protection against discharge diseases, such as gonorrhea, chlamydia, and trichomoniasis. Since half of all sexually transmitted infections (estimated at 18.9 million annually) occur in people under age 25, downplaying condoms' effectiveness is both illogical and dangerous.

The Claim: Contraception is unreliable and ineffective.

The Facts: When used consistently and correctly, contraception can be extremely effective at preventing unwanted pregnancies. While a typical woman who uses no method of contraception has an 85 percent chance of becoming pregnant in one year, women who regularly use contraception have a much lower chance of pregnancy. Failure rates for various contraceptive methods range from .05 percent over a year for the contraceptive implant (Implanon), to three percent for Depo-Provera ("the shot"), and eight percent for the patch, ring, and birth control pills, up to 16 percent for the diaphragm, and 29 percent for spermicides used alone (without a condom or other method).

CHAPTER 3

Personal Narratives

A Young Woman Survives HPV and Cancer

Joslyn

In the following viewpoint a young woman named Joslyn recounts a scary time in her life when she found out she had HPV and, later, cervical cancer. She survived both and is living life to the fullest. She wants other women to become educated about HPV and cervical cancer.

Joslyn posted her story on the website of Tamika & Friends, a national nonprofit organization dedicated to raising awareness of HPV and its link to cancer. The organization was founded by cervical cancer survivor Tamika Felder.

I was getting ready to start my first year of college, moving into the dorms and finally moving out of my parent's house—FREEDOM—but before I could do all of that my mom asked if I could get a pap and physical done for the life insurance policy. I thought nothing of it, until a week later I received a call from my doctor

Photo on facing page. A pathology lab technician analyzes a cervical pap smear for signs of cancer. (© National Cancer Institute/Photo Researchers, Inc.)

asking me to come in to re-do the pap because they had discovered abnormal cells in my test which could indicate CANCER. . . . I remember I was home with my mom just about to leave the house to pick up new bedding. I immediately dropped the phone and began to cry. My mom had to pick up the receiver and continue the conversation. We made an appointment for later that week. The next few days and weeks blew by until I received the next call that I had HPV and not to worry because in most women HPV will go away on its own. I was asked to come back every 6 months to re-do the pap. I was so relieved, but little did I know this was just the beginning. After going to about what felt like 100 paps the HPV cells were not going away. I began to get frustrated and concerned. The doctor again told me not to worry, that these things just take time.

> **FAST FACT**
>
> When detected at an early stage, the five-year survival rate for women with invasive cervical cancer is 91 percent, according to Cancer.net.

Learning the Realities of HPV

During my sophomore year of college I took a Reproductive Biology class to fulfill my credit and during that class the professor decided to discuss HPV and the rising number of women affected by this disease. I couldn't believe the information that was never conveyed to me, that the little cell I had in me might not go away—that it might grow into cancer. I decided to do more research on HPV and went straight to the library, pulling every article or book I could find on HPV. After about 10 hours of research and a research paper complete, I made an appointment with a new OBGYN [doctor of obstetrics and gynecology] and with research in hand asked my new doctor for new options. I got a copo [colposcopy, an examination of the cervix using a magnifying device called a colposcope, followed by a biopsy if warranted; it can also be used to cut out cancerous cells] done to remove the cells and asked to get the cells tested. The test came

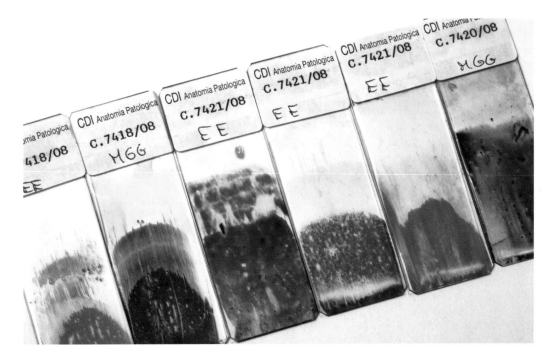

back that I had the high risk strain and about 10 different types of HPV. Skipping 2 years . . . I met the man of my life, graduated college, and thought my life was fulfilled, until IT came back. At 22, after a weekend in Vegas for my Bachelorette party, I received a message from my OB that the HPV cell had now grown into stage 1 cancer. I was crushed, to say the least. My future husband and I called the doctor to schedule a follow-up appointment to discuss treatment options. Since I was getting married in 2 months the doctors suggested I wait until after the wedding to schedule the cone biopsy. In August of 2006 I married the love of my life . . . went on an amazing honeymoon . . . and then in September I went in to have the cells removed. I am happy to say now that I have had 3 years of negative paps and loving every minute of life. I know this is a long story, but please know you are not alone and that learning about HPV and cervical cancer can make a difference. Get your pap and empower yourself and your friends and family with the facts.

These Pap smear slides will be examined under a microscope. Getting regular Pap smears helps girls and women detect the early signs of cervical cancer. (© Mauro Fermariello/ Photo Researchers, Inc.)

A Grandmother Wants Her Grandchildren to Get the HPV Vaccination

Susie Wilson

In the following viewpoint Susie Wilson explains the issues behind the HPV vaccine and why she wants her grandchildren to get vaccinated. According to Wilson, she did not think too much about the HPV vaccine until the US Centers for Disease Control and Prevention recommended that boys get vaccinated. Then, says the grandmother of three boys and one girl, she researched the issue and became supportive of the vaccine. She hopes all her grandchildren will receive it.

Wilson is a senior adviser for Answer, a national organization dedicated to providing and promoting comprehensive sexuality education to young people and the adults who teach them.

In 2010, when Gardasil—the human papillomavirus ... (HPV) vaccine for girls as young as nine—was approved by the U.S. Food and Drug Administration [FDA], I dropped the news into my subconscious and forgot about it. With only one granddaughter to call my own, then nine-years-old, I just didn't want to face the fact [that] someday she would be sexually active and need protection against HPV, a sexually transmitted disease [STD] that can cause cervical cancer and genital warts.

But last month [October 2011], when a federal advisory committee with the Centers for Disease Control and Prevention [CDC] recommended that boys and young men, nine to 21, should be vaccinated with Gardasil, like Snow White, I woke up.

Waking Up to the HPV Debate

All at once, I focused foursquare on the current debate over whether boys and girls should receive the vaccine, a series of three shots. If so, they could be protected against different cancers caused by four strains of the HPV virus that can develop in adulthood from sexual contact that occurred at younger ages.

I have three grandsons who fall into the suggested age range for the vaccine and one, at age eight, who is on the cusp. My granddaughter will be 11 in March. They are in the crosshairs of the debate. I am not these children's parents, but I'm their grandmother who writes about sexual health issues. So I decided to act after the committee's announcement.

Fortunately for me, I have a pediatrician in the family (my son-in-law). When I asked him whether he would have his two sons vaccinated, he connected me to a colleague of his with expertise in the area. He said based on what she recommended, and in consultation with his wife, [he would] then decide about vaccinating his two sons.

His colleague Lydia A. Shrier . . . , attending physician in adolescent/young adult medicine at Boston's Children's Hospital and associate professor of pediatrics at the Harvard Medical School, kindly answered my questions on the vaccine, its importance, its efficacy, and her recommendations to parents.

I asked her via e-mail for her best reason to convince parents to have their daughters and sons vaccinated when they are young.

"Vaccination is one of the most important public health initiatives, and saves countless lives, considerable suffering, and many dollars," Dr. Shrier replied.

"[Gardasil] is only helpful for people who haven't acquired the [four] HPV types protected by the vaccine, which is why it is recommended for girls and boys at age 11 to 12 (hopefully before they have had any kind of sexual contact that would result in HPV transmission)."

While it may be hard to believe, Dr. Shrier noted that most people who ever have sexual contact will be infected with at least one type of HPV, with many becoming infected with multiple types.

Yet despite the facts, some are against youth getting the vaccine, fearing that it will give them a license to be sexually active. I asked Dr. Shrier to respond to the charge[:]

"The decision to have sexual contact is a complex, personal decision. There is no evidence that the preventive health recommendation for the HPV vaccine influences that decision.

"The HPV vaccine works best for abstinent individuals and is offered along with other preventive health measures, including supporting abstinence for our pediatric patients who have not yet had sex," she added.

I would add that if parents decide to vaccinate their children, they may use it as a teachable moment to talk to their 11- to 14-year-olds not once but often about the many good reasons to choose abstinence and avoid risky sexual behaviors like intercourse.

Parents can also teach their kids about what the vaccine does not do: protect against unplanned pregnancy and other STDs.

I asked Dr. Shrier to give parents tips on starting the conversation about getting Gardasil with their kids. She said they should talk about it in an age-appropriate way: "These shots will help your body to be protected against infection from types of a virus, HPV, which can make you sick with warts or cancer."

They might add: "You get exposed to HPV through sexual contact, so it is very important that you have this protection in your system before the time in your life when you have this contact."

Some parents oppose vaccinations for their children; one group in particular believes that vaccinations cause autism. I asked Dr. Shrier to comment on whether there was a vaccine/autism link. She was quick to discredit that one:

"The question of vaccines and autism has been examined extensively; there is no evidence that vaccines cause autism."

After Dr. Shrier's advice, I thought again about why I had neglected to talk to my daughter about having my granddaughter vaccinated with Gardasil. I believe my reason was that it was only offered to females, in this case young girls. Once again, the burden of responsibility about sexual health was placed on their shoulders.

Throughout history, choosing abstinence, using contraception, and protecting against STDs have been traditionally seen as "women's issues." Men got off easily when it came to accepting responsibility for their or their partners' sexual well-being.

Now that Gardasil has also been recommended for boys and young men, the playing field is more even (at least in this one area of sexual health)—and I feel much better about recommending Gardasil for all my grandchildren.

I hope sexuality educators incorporate discussion about the good reasons for the vaccine in late elementary and middle school, so that students will understand

> **FAST FACT**
>
> Since 2004 cervical cancer rates have decreased by 2.1 percent per year in women younger than fifty years of age and by 3.1 percent per year in women fifty and older, according to the American Cancer Society.

its importance. Smart school administrators might hold parent sessions about Gardasil and invite local pediatricians to speak about why both girls and boys should receive it.

As for this grandmother, I feel good just having more information to send to my own children and my son-in-law, the doctor. I hope it will help them make a good decision for their children. If I could tell them one thing, it is this:

"Have your kids vaccinated against cancers caused by HPV; it's a no-brainer."

Men Can Get HPV, Too

"SADD"

In the following viewpoint a member of the group HPV Hope, calling himself Seattlelite Against Disease and Deception, or "SADD," discusses having HPV from a man's perspective. According to "SADD," HPV gave him anal warts. He advises others to avoid the embarrassment, the pain of having them removed, and the potential to spread them to your partner and advises men to protect themselves from HPV by wearing a condom during sex.

HPV Hope is a Seattle-based volunteer organization offering monthly HPV support groups.

HPV. Forget all the medical mumbo jumbo—it's warts and they suck. All you hear about is women getting them. Cervical cancer, get your daughters vaccinated for the virus. But another part of it you don't hear about is men getting them. Fortunately I haven't had the warts on my man parts, although I've heard of men who had. Not only would that be embarrassing but really painful. I've had them on my, well, I'll just say it, anus. They are extremely painful and even more painful to get rid of. Here's a quick little story of how it happened.

Finding Out I Had HPV

One day I noticed that my butt was itching—in that certain area. I gave it up to hemorrhoids, got some cream and waited. However when putting the cream on I felt bumps. I didn't pay any attention because honestly who spends time touching their anus to see what it feels like? Well the itching got worse and worse. Eventually one day it began to bleed from wiping after going to the bathroom. I went to Harborview STD Clinic [in Seattle] and had it checked out. The news was weird to hear—you have anal warts. What the heck are anal warts? How did I get them? I'd recently broken up with a boyfriend of one year and was starting to date another guy. I'd always been safe—condoms and all. The doctor told me I had HPV. She explained that the kind of warts I had were pretty normal—80% of the sexually active population has them. However they can cause major problems if not taken care of—cancers, sterility and more. I was shocked. The doctor put me at ease and then said here comes the fun part. She brought out a canister of nitrous [liquid nitrogen] and said alright, bend over and we'll burn them off. BURN them off??? Yes. Burn. It was incredibly painful and extremely embarrassing. Nothing like having a doctor's face right in your butt burning warts off your anus.

It's been 7 years now and I haven't had another outbreak. Thank goodness. Although, every time it itches down there I get nervous. I can't tell you how many times I've gone back to the STD clinic and they've always told

> **FAST FACT**
>
> Each year in the United States about four hundred men will get HPV-associated penile cancer and fifteen hundred men will get HPV-associated anal cancer, according to the US Centers for Disease Control and Prevention.

me—you're fine, you have hemorrhoids, quit worrying. But let me tell you—after you've had them burned off, you do not want them again. Unfortunately there's no testing for them. They don't show up on any screening for STD tests. The only way to know if you have them is to feel down there, or go to the doctor every time you are itching and think you might have them.

All I can say is—ALWAYS wear a condom. You do not want to have to go through all of the pain and embarrassment that anal warts and HPV causes. If you're gay—you don't want to pass them onto a partner. If you're straight—you definitely don't want to give them to your girlfriend/wife. Passing it onto women is worse because they can get cervical cancer among other things. So, be safe, be clean and be smart. There's no other way to put it—you don't want them. Besides—it takes a couple seconds to put a condom on. It takes a life time to deal with HPV.

The author says that men must be safe, be clean, and be smart about sexually transmitted diseases such as HPV by always using a condom during sexual activity.
(© Jonathan A. Mayers/ Stock Connection Distribution/Alamy)

GLOSSARY

acellular Not made up of cells or divided into cells.

adenocarcinoma A cancer that develops in the lining or inner surface of an organ that usually has glandular (secreting) properties.

ASC-US (atypical squamous cells of undetermined significance) Medical term for an inconclusive Pap test. The squamous cells of the cervix do not look entirely normal but do not look entirely abnormal either.

asymptomatic Having no symptoms.

biopsy Removal of a sample of tissue that is then examined under a microscope to confirm whether abnormal cells, including cancer, are present.

Cervarix An HPV vaccine directed at two HPV types, 16 and 18, produced by GlaxoSmithKline.

cervical dysplasia A term that refers to abnormal changes in the cells on the surface of the cervix.

cervix The Latin word for "neck," in anatomy it refers to the lower, cylindrical end of the uterus that connects to the vagina.

CIN (cervical intraepithelial neoplasia) General term used to describe the growth of abnormal cells on the surface of the cervix. Numbers from 1 to 3 (as in CIN 1 or CIN 3) are used to describe the degree of abnormal changes that have developed.

clinical HPV The presence of warts and precancerous changes on the external genitalia that usually can be seen with the naked eye.

colposcopy A medical procedure in which the vagina and the surface of the cervix are examined under magnification using a lighted scope (colposcope) to detect the presence of precancerous cells or cancer.

PERSPECTIVES ON DISEASES AND DISORDERS

condylomata acuminata	The term used to describe an HPV wart when it is raised and cauliflower-shaped (papillary). Most of these kinds of warts are caused by so-called low-risk (noncarcinogenic) HPV 6 or 11.
condyloma planum	The term used to describe HPV warts that are flat. These warts are generally associated with HPV 16 or other "high-risk" types.
cryosurgery	Treatment to destroy abnormal tissue, such as a wart, using an instrument that freezes the targeted cells.
cytology	The medical term for a cell test or study, such as a Pap test.
epithelial	Referring to the epithelium, the layer of cells forming the epidermis of the skin and the surface layer of mucous membranes.
false negative	A test result that appears normal, but in reality is not. In the case of a Pap test, this occurs when cervical cells examined in the lab are mistakenly interpreted as healthy, thus allowing abnormalities to progress unchecked.
false positive	A test result that appears abnormal, but in reality is not. In the case of a Pap test, this occurs when cervical cells examined in the lab are mistakenly interpreted as abnormal, thus making additional tests necessary and causing patient anxiety.
Gardasil	An HPV vaccine produced by Merck & Co., also referred to as the quadrivalent HPV vaccine because it protects against four HPV types (6, 11, 16, and 18).
genital warts	Warts on the vagina, vulva, cervix, or penis caused by HPV.
genitourinary cancers	Cancers affecting the reproductive organs or urinary tract, including bladder, kidney, penile, prostate, testicular, and urethral cancers.
gynecology	The field of medicine that focuses on the care of the female reproductive system.
high-risk HPV	Strains of HPV, such as HPV 16 and 18, that are associated with a high risk of developing cancer.
HPV DNA test	A laboratory test in which cells are scraped from the cervix and analyzed for the presence of HPV genetic material.

HSIL (high-grade squamous intraepithelial lesion)	Moderate to severe dysplasia (precancerous cervical cells), also called CIN 2 or CIN 3, which is diagnosed using a colposcopy and biopsy.
human papillomavirus (HPV)	A group of about a hundred types of DNA-containing viruses that cause warts and certain cancers and precancers of the skin lining the lower genital tract, anus, throat, and mouth.
hysterectomy	An operation in which the uterus is removed, often including the cervix.
latent HPV infection	HPV infection that cannot be detected by visual inspection, cytology, or even by HPV testing. Individuals with latent HPV are not contagious.
lesion	Any abnormal tissue, usually caused by disease or trauma.
loop electrosurgical excision procedure (LEEP)	A procedure that removes or destroys precancerous tissue without removing or altering the surrounding tissues.
low-grade squamous intraepithelial lesion (LSIL)	Mildly abnormal cells, also called CIN 1, diagnosed using a colposcopy and sometimes a biopsy. In most cases, these types of abnormal cervical cells go away on their own without treatment.
low-risk HPV	Strains of HPV, such as HPV 6 and HPV 11, which are virtually never found in cancers and thus are also called noncarcinogenic HPV types.
oncogenic	Promoting the formation or development of cancer.
oncologist	A doctor who specializes in treating cancer.
oropharynx	The middle part of the pharynx (throat) behind the mouth; includes the back one-third of the tongue, the soft palate, the side and back walls of the throat, and the tonsils.
papilloma	A benign wart.
Pap test	A test in which a sample of cervical cells collected during a gynecologic exam is looked at under a microscope for signs of abnormalities. It is named after Dr. George Papanicolaou, who first developed the test.

pathologist	A doctor who diagnoses disease by studying cells and tissue under a microscope.
photodynamic therapy (PDT)	A treatment for tumors in which a light-sensitive dye is injected into the blood (or skin) to be taken up selectively by the tumors. Light of a specific wavelength is then applied to the affected area to kill the tumors.
podophyllin	A topical drug used to treat genital warts.
precancerous	Cells or tissue that are not currently cancerous, but may become so over time without treatment.
prophylactic	Something that prevents or defends against an infection.
reflex HPV testing	An HPV test that is performed on a sample of cervical cells following an inconclusive Pap test (also called an ASC-US Pap).
sexually transmitted disease (STD)	A viral or bacterial infection passed between two persons during sexual activity.
squamous cell carcinoma	Cancer of the squamous cells, a type of cell in the epithelium, found in the skin and the linings of many tissues in the body. Squamous cell carcinoma is the most common type of cervical cancer.
strain	A genetic variant or subtype of a virus or bacterium.
subclinical HPV infection	Applies to HPV-induced changes in the skin cells of the lower genital tract that cannot be seen with the naked eye.
vagina	The muscular "canal" that extends from the cervix to the outside of the body. Its opening is located between the urethra (where urine exits the body) and the anus. Also called the birth canal.
vulva	The external female genitals. The vulva includes the pubic mound, labia (lips), clitoris, and vaginal opening.

CHRONOLOGY

1907 Human papillomas (warts) are linked to an infectious agent.

1911 American pathologist Peyton Rous discovers that viruses can cause cancer.

1920s American doctor George Papanicolaou develops a technique to examine vaginal smears under a microscope and begins using it to detect uterine cancer. The technique would come to be known as the Pap test or Pap smear.

1930s Richard Shope, a medical doctor and researcher from Iowa, isolates a strain of the papillomavirus that causes horn-like warts on infected rabbits.

1943 Papanicolaou publishes the book *Diagnosis of Uterine Cancer by the Vaginal Smear.*

1950s Widespread use of the Pap smear begins.

1975 German scientist Harold zur Hausen finds evidence linking the human papillomavirus (HPV) with cervical cancer.

1979 Hausen and his associates successfully isolate and clone the first HPV DNA from genital warts, HPV-6 (a non-carcinogenic type).

1983 HPV-16 (a high-risk HPV type) is successfully isolated and cloned by Hausen and his associates.

1990s   Scientists at Georgetown University, the University of Rochester, the National Cancer Institute, and Queensland University in Australia make key discoveries that lead to the development of the HPV vaccine.

1995   The World Health Organization and the International Agency for Research on Cancer identify HPV as the major cause of cervical cancer and cervical dysplasia.

2002   A study published in the *New England Journal of Medicine* finds that the HPV vaccine Gardasil, made by Merck, is effective in preventing cervical cancer.

2004   A study is published in the *Lancet* showing the effectiveness of Cervarix, the HPV vaccine made by GlaxoSmithKline.

2006   The US Food and Drug Administration (FDA) approves Gardasil for use in females, and the US Centers for Disease Control and Prevention (CDC) recommend that all girls and women aged eleven to twenty-six receive the vaccine.

2008   Hausen receives the Nobel Prize in Physiology or Medicine for his discovery that HPV causes cervical cancer.

2009   The FDA approves Cervarix, and the CDC recommends its use in females. The FDA also approves the use of Gardasil in males.

2011   The CDC recommends that Gardasil be used routinely in males.

ORGANIZATIONS TO CONTACT

The editors have compiled the following list of organizations concerned with the issues debated in this book. The descriptions are derived from materials provided by the organizations. All have publications or information available for interested readers. The list was compiled on the date of publication of the present volume; the information provided here may change. Be aware that many organizations take several weeks or longer to respond to inquiries, so allow as much time as possible.

American Cancer Society (ACS)
1599 Clifton Rd. NE, Atlanta, GA 30329
(800) 227-2345; fax: (404) 329-5787
e-mail: www.cancer
.org/asp/contactUs
/cus_global.asp
website: www.cancer
.org

The ACS is a nationwide, community-based, voluntary health organization dedicated to eliminating cancer as a major health problem through research, education, advocacy, and service. The ACS publishes three peer-reviewed scientific periodicals, *CA: A Cancer Journal for Clinicians, Cancer,* and *Cancer Cytopathology.*

American College of Obstetricians and Gynecologists (ACOG)
409 Twelfth St. SW, PO Box 96920, Washington, DC 20090-6920
(202) 638-5577
website: www.acog.org

The ACOG is a nonprofit organization of professionals providing health care for women. It advocates for quality health care for women, promotes patient education, and increases awareness among its members and the public of the changing issues facing women's health care. ACOG issues important guidelines and bulletins and publishes several journals, including *Obstetrics & Gynecology* and *Special Issues in Women's Health.*

American Social Health Association (ASHA)
PO Box 13827, Research Triangle Park, NC 27709
(919) 361-8400; fax: (919) 361-8425
e-mail: info@ashastd .org
website: www.ashastd .org

ASHA is a nonprofit organization dedicated to improving the health of individuals, families, and communities, with an emphasis on sexual health and a focus on preventing sexually transmitted diseases and their harmful consequences. Toward this goal, ASHA created the National HPV and Cervical Cancer Prevention Resource Center to provide cervical cancer prevention information and resources. The center provides accurate and up-to-date information about HPV and cervical cancer prevention and related issues, such as screening, self-esteem, partners, and transmission.

American Society for Colposcopy and Cervical Pathology (ASCCP)
1530 Tilco Dr., Ste. C, Frederick, MD 21704
(800) 787-7227; fax: (301) 733-5775
e-mail: administrator @asccp.org
website: www.asccp.org

The ASCCP is an organization of health care professionals who study, diagnose, and treat HPV, cervical cancer, and other lower genital tract disorders. It provides education and seeks to improve clinician competence and performance and patient outcomes in the field of lower genital tract disorders. The ASCCP publishes the monthly *Journal of Lower Genital Tract Disease.*

EngenderHealth
440 Ninth Ave., New York, NY 10001
(212) 561-8000
e-mail: info@engender health.org
website: www.engender health.org

EngenderHealth is a nonprofit organization dedicated to increasing access to reproductive health care around the world. The organization promotes gender equity, advocates for sound practices and policies, and inspires people to assert their rights to better, healthier lives. The organization does this by sharing its expertise in sexual and reproductive health with local organizations in more than twenty different countries. EngenderHealth is a member organization of the Alliance for Cervical Cancer Prevention (ACCP). Within the ACCP, EngenderHealth plays a key role in studying the safety and efficacy of HPV screening and treatment technologies and in developing appropriate, sustainable service delivery approaches. EngenderHealth publishes a wide range of materials, including training curricula, clinical guidelines, instructional videos, brochures, working papers, articles, and online information.

Foundation for Women's Cancer
230 W. Monroe St., Ste. 2528, Chicago, IL 60606
(312) 578-1439; fax: (312) 578-9769
e-mail: info@foundationforwomenscancer.org
website: www.wcn.org

The Foundation for Women's Cancer is a nonprofit organization dedicated to funding research and training and ensuring education and public awareness of gynecologic cancer prevention, early detection, and optimal treatment. Toward these goals, the foundation provides education about gynecologic cancers; supports promising, innovative gynecologic cancer research; and trains a cadre of clinicians/scientists to participate in clinically relevant research in collaboration with the National Cancer Institute. The organization provides many brochures and other resources about women's cancer, including the *Women's Cancer Bulletin* and the *State of the State of Gynecologic Cancers.*

HPV and Anal Cancer Foundation
PO Box 232, New York, NY 10272
(646) 593-7739
e-mail: info@analcancerfoundation.org
website: http://analcancerfoundation.org

The HPV and Anal Cancer Foundation is a national public service organization dedicated to reducing suffering of and ensuring quality care for those affected by anal cancer and HPV. Specifically, the foundation aims to raise awareness about HPV-related cancers, provide support to patients, and encourage funding for research into HPV and cancer. The organization's website provides information and patient stories.

National Cancer Institute (NCI)
NCI Public Inquiries Office, 6116 Executive Blvd., Rm. 3036A, Bethesda, MD 20892
(800) 422-6237
e-mail: www.cancer.gov/global/contact/email-us
website: www.cancer.gov

The NCI is one of the twenty-seven institutes and centers that constitute the National Institutes of Health. The NCI coordinates the National Cancer Program, which conducts and supports research, training, health information dissemination, and other programs with respect to the cause, diagnosis, prevention, and treatment of cancer, rehabilitation from cancer, and the continuing care of cancer patients and the families of cancer patients. The NCI conducts research in its own laboratories and clinics and collaborates with voluntary organizations and other national and foreign institutions engaged in cancer research and training activities. The institute publishes a biweekly newsletter, the *NCI Cancer Bulletin,* to provide useful, timely information about cancer research.

National Center for HIV/AIDS, Viral Hepatitis, STD, and TB Prevention (NCHHSTP)
US Centers for Disease Control and Prevention
1600 Clifton Rd.,
Mailstop G-37,
Atlanta, GA 30333
(404) 718-8500;
fax: (404) 718-8588
e-mail: cdcinfo@cdc.gov
website: www.cdc.gov /hpv

The NCHHSTP is part of the Centers for Disease Control and Prevention (CDC), an agency of the US Department of Health and Human Services. The NCHHSTP maximizes public health and safety nationally and internationally through the elimination, prevention, and control of disease, disability, and death caused by communicable diseases, including HPV, HIV/AIDS, viral hepatitis, and other sexually transmitted diseases. The CDC's HPV website provides information about HPV, including information geared to patients, educators, and health professionals.

National Vaccine Information Center (NVIC)
407 Church St., Ste. H, Vienna, VA 22180
(703) 938-0342;
fax: (703) 938-5768
e-mail: contactnvic @gmail.com
website: www.nvic.org

The NVIC is a national nonprofit organization dedicated to the prevention of vaccine injuries and deaths through public education and to defending the informed consent ethic in medicine. The NVIC acts as an independent clearinghouse for information on diseases and vaccines and supports the availability of all preventive health care options, including vaccines, and the right of consumers to make educated, voluntary health care choices.

Oral Cancer Foundation (OCF)
3419 Via Lido #205, Newport Beach, CA 92663
(949) 646-8000
e-mail: info@oral cancerfoundation.org
website: http://oral cancerfoundation.org

The OCF is a nonprofit, public service charity designed for advocacy and service. It was created to promote change, through proactive means, in both the public and medical/dental professional sectors. At the forefront of the organization's agenda is publicizing the need to undergo an annual oral cancer screening, combined with an outreach to the dental and medical communities to provide this service as a matter of routine practice. The OCF provides information about the connection between oral cancer and HPV infection and offers articles and patient stories about oral cancer in a monthly newsletter.

Planned Parenthood Federation of America
434 W. Thirty-Third St., New York, NY 10001
(212) 541-7800; fax: (212) 245-1845
website: www.planned parenthood.org

Planned Parenthood is a nonprofit organization dedicated to reproductive health. It delivers reproductive health care, sex education, and information to women, men, and young people around the world. Planned Parenthood provides information for teens, parents, and educators about HPV and other sexually transmitted diseases on its website.

Tamika & Friends
PO Box 2942, Upper Marlboro, MD 20773
(866) 595-2448
website: www.tamika andfriends.org

Tamika & Friends, Inc. is a national nonprofit organization dedicated to raising awareness about cervical cancer and its link to HPV. The organization was founded by and named after cervical cancer survivor Tamika Felder. The organization supports women with cervical cancer and seeks to eliminate the disease through education, prevention, and treatment.

FOR FURTHER READING

Books   Bonnie Diraimondo, *Any Mother's Daughter: One Woman's Lifelong Struggle with HPV*. Bloomington, IN: AuthorHouse, 2010.

Don Dizon and Michael Krychman, *Questions & Answers About Human Papilloma Virus (HPV)*. Sudbury, MA: Jones & Bartlett, 2010.

Jill Grimes, *Seductive Delusions: How Everyday People Catch STDs*. Baltimore: Johns Hopkins University Press, 2008.

Shobha Krishnan, *The HPV Vaccine Controversy: Sex, Cancer, God, and Politics: A Guide for Parents, Women, Men and Teenagers*. Westport, CT: Praeger, 2008.

Hans Krueger, Gavin Stuart, Richard Gallagher, Dan Williams, and Jon Kerner, *HPV and Other Infectious Agents in Cancer: Opportunities for Prevention and Public Health*. New York: Oxford University Press, 2010.

Ilana Löwy, *A Woman's Disease: The History of Cervical Cancer*. Oxford: Oxford University Press, 2011.

Adina Nack, *Damaged Goods? Women Living with Incurable Sexually Transmitted Diseases*. Philadelphia: Temple University Press, 2008.

Jane Semple, *HPV and Cervical Dysplasia: A Naturopathic Approach*. Orem, UT: Woodland, 2007.

David Servan-Schreiber, *Anticancer: A New Way of Life*. New York: Viking, 2009.

Rebecca Skloot, *The Immortal Life of Henrietta Lacks*. New York: Crown, 2010.

Keith Wailoo et al., eds., *Three Shots at Prevention: The HPV Vaccine and the Politics of Medicine's Simple Solutions*. Baltimore: Johns Hopkins University Press, 2010.

Periodicals and Internet Sources

Nathan Wolfe, *The Viral Storm: The Dawn of a New Pandemic Age.* New York: Times, 2011.

J.D. Allen et al., "Decision-Making About the HPV Vaccine Among Ethnically Diverse Parents: Implications for Health Communications," *Journal of Oncology*, 2012.

Lux Alptraum, "The HPV Vaccine's Misguided Scare Tactics," *Jezebel*, May 11, 2010. http://jezebel.com/5535380/the-hpv-vaccines-misguided-scare-tactics.

Darla Carter, "Cervical Cancer: There's an App for That," *USA Today*, February 2, 2012.

Amanda Chan, " HPV Vaccine Sees Poor Completion Rates," MyHealthNewsDaily, November 10, 2010. www.myhealthnews daily.com/495-hpv-vaccine-sees-poor-completion-rates.html.

Anil K. Chaturvedi, "Beyond Cervical Cancer: Burden of Other HPV-Related Cancers Among Men and Women," *Journal of Adolescent Health*, April 2010.

Bonnie Diraimondo, "The Connection Between Lupus and HPV-Cancers," EmpowHER, October 10, 2011. www.empow her.com/cancer/content/connection-between-lupus-and-hpv -cancers.

Ernesto Domingues, "The Role of 'Men' in Preventing HPV Related Cervical Cancer!," Chatmosphere, January 11, 2012. http://chatpdx.org/2012/01/11/the-role-of-men-in-preventing -hpv-related-cervical-cancer/.

Guttmacher Institute, "Facts on American Teens' Sexual and Reproductive Health," February 2012. www.guttmacher.org /pubs/FB-ATSRH.html.

Martha Kempner, "Vaccinating Children Is a Social Responsi-bility We Can Not Afford to Shirk," RH Reality Check, January 3, 2012. www.rhrealitycheck.org/article/2012/01/03/vaccinating -children-against-diseases-including-hpv-is-one-our-societal -responsib.

Richard Knox, "Why HPV Vaccination of Boys May Be Easier," *Shots* (blog), National Public Radio, November 7, 2011. www .npr.org/blogs/health/2011/11/07/142030282/why-hpv-vaccina tion-of-boys-may-be-easier.

Rachel Levy, "Study: Fewer Girls Are Getting Necessary Doses of HPV Vaccine," *Slate*, May 3, 2012. http://slatest.slate.com /posts/2012/05/03/fewer_girls_receiving_all_three_doses_of _hpv_vaccine.html.

Marilynn Marchione, "Black Women Have Trouble Clearing Cervical Cancer Virus," *USA Today*, April 1, 2012.

Melody McCloud, "HPV Linked to Heart Disease in Women, Oral Sex and Cancer in Men—Well, Shut Yo' Mouth!," *Psychology Today*, 2011.

Barbara Meltz, "Should Your Teen Get the HPV Vaccine?," *Moms* (blog), Boston.com, March 29, 2010. www.boston.com /community/moms/blogs/child_caring/2010/03/should_your _teen_get_the_hpv_vaccine.html.

Regina Nuzzo, "Replacing the Pap Smear?," *CR Magazine*, Summer 2009.

Beth W. Orenstein, "The Link Between HPV and Non-Cervical Cancers," Everydayhealth, January 14, 2011. www.everyday health.com/sexual-health/the-link-between-hpv-and-non -cervical-cancers.aspx.

Darci Picoult, "I Had the Cancer No One Talks About," *Redbook*, June 2011.

Roni Caryn Rabin, "Saving Lives from Anal Cancer," *New York Times*, February 9, 2011.

Karly Rossiter, "I Sued My Ex for Giving Me an STI," *Cleo*, March 1, 2011.

Karen Rowan, "HPV May Raise Women's Risk of Heart Disease," MyHealthNewsDaily, October 25, 2011. www.myhealthnewsdaily .com/1824-hpv-raises-womens-risk-heart-disease .html.

Jacob Sullum, "Harris Poll Reflects and Reinforces Incoherent Thinking About 'Public Health,'" *Reason*, March 21, 2012.

Leigh Vinocur, "HPV from Oral Sex? Young People Often Underestimate the Risk," *Huffington Post*, April 19, 2011. www.huffingtonpost.com/leigh-vinocur-md/oral-sex-cancer _b_850066.html.

Patrice Wendling, "HPV-Related Oral Cancer Incidence Spikes Sharply," *Oncology Report*, June 4, 2011.

INDEX

A

Abstinence-only sex education
  is ineffective, 98–107
  prevents sexually transmitted diseases,
    89–97
ACIP (Advisory Committee on
  Immunization Practices), 67–68, 78, 79,
  83
ACOG (American College of Obstetricians
  and Gynecologists), 9–10
ACPeds (American College of
  Pediatricians), 89
ACS (American Cancer Society), 10, 11,
  115
Advisory Committee on Immunization
  Practices (ACIP), 67–68, 78, 79, 83
Advocates for Youth, 98, 100
American Cancer Society (ACS), 10, 11,
  115
American College of Obstetricians and
  Gynecologists (ACOG), 9–10
American College of Pediatricians
  (ACPeds), 89
American Journal of Preventive Medicine,
  84–85
Anal cancer, 16
  among gay/bisexual men, 81
  annual incidence of, *70, 73*
    among men, 118
  efficacy of HPV vaccine in preventing,
    74–75
Answer, 112
Axe, Josh, 50

B

Bachmann, Michele, 58, *58*, 62, 68

Bassett, Laura, 58
BCA (bichloroacetic acid), 37
Birth rates, teen, 102
Boys. *See* Men/boys
Brehany, John F., 78
Burchell, Ann, 27, 28

C

Cancers
  HPV-related, incidence of, *73*
  percentages caused by high-risk types of
    HPV, 18
  See also Anal cancer; Cervical cancer;
    Oropharyngeal cancers; Penile cancer
Catholic Medical Association (CMA), 79
Centers for Disease Control and
  Prevention, US (CDC), 32, 44
  HIV prevention efforts of, 105
  on anal cancer among gay/bisexual men,
    81
  on annual new HPV infections, 40
  on cost of STDs to health care system, 91
  on number of HPV vaccine doses
    administered in US, 47
  on prevalence of anal/penile cancers, 118
  on prevalence of genital warts among
    sexually active men, 74
  on prevalence of HPV infections, 16, 51,
    52
  on rates of oropharyngeal cancers, 69
  on STDs among adults *vs.* youth, 90
  See also Advisory Committee on
    Immunization Practices
Cervarix (vaccine), 25, *46*
  cost of, 79
  numbers participating in trials of, 45